— tw

per w

is charge

due ks.

God's Kingdom

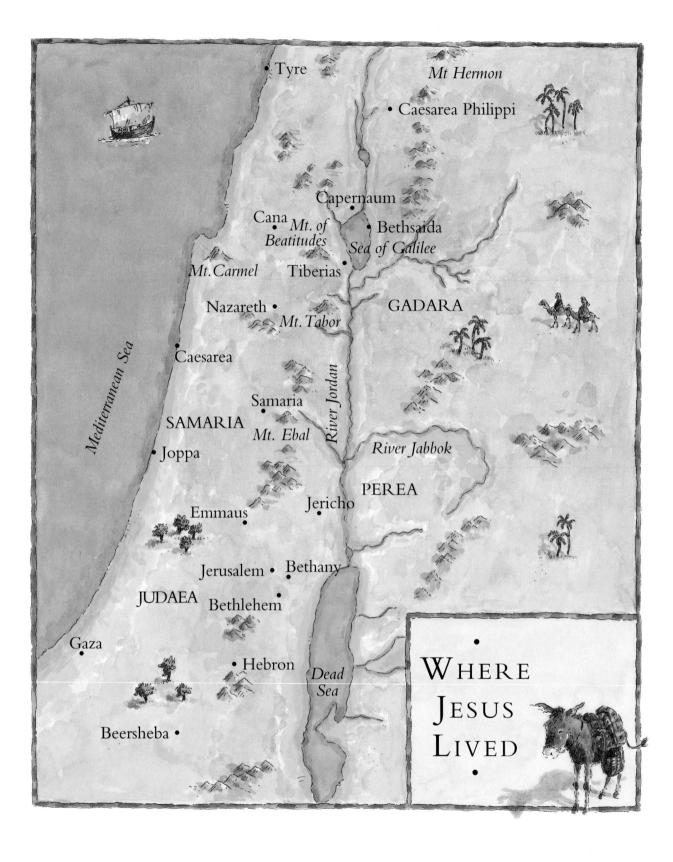

Tyre

Mt Hermon

Caesarea Philippi

Capernaum

Cana
Mt. of
Beatitudes

Bethsaida
Sea of Galilee

Mt. Carmel

Tiberias

GADARA

Nazareth

Mt. Tabor

Mediterranean Sea

Caesarea

Samaria

SAMARIA

River Jordan

Mt. Ebal

River Jabbok

Joppa

PEREA

Emmaus

Jericho

Jerusalem

Bethany

JUDAEA

Bethlehem

Gaza

Hebron

Dead
Sea

Beersheba

WHERE
JESUS
LIVED

God's Kingdom

STORIES FROM THE
NEW TESTAMENT

Retold by
GERALDINE
McCAUGHREAN

Illustrated by
ANNA C. LEPLAR

Orion Children's Books
and

Picture Dolphins

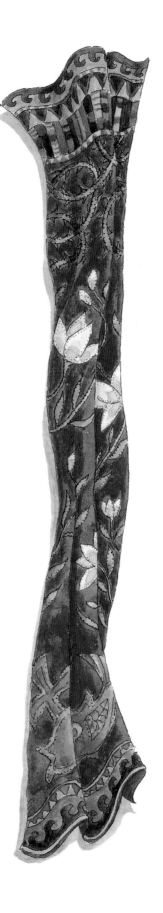

To Lucy and Rod
G.M.

To Chloë and Simon
A.C.L.

Also by Geraldine McCaughrean

Stories from Shakespeare

God's People

Myths and Legends of the World:
The Golden Hoard
The Silver Treasure
The Bronze Cauldron
The Crystal Pool

First published in Great Britain in 1999
by Orion Children's Books
a division of the Orion Publishing Group Ltd
Orion House
5 Upper St Martin's Lane
London WC2H 9EA

Text copyright © Geraldine McCaughrean 1999
Illustrations copyright © Anna C. Leplar 1999
Designed by Dalia Hartman

A catalogue record for this book is available from the British Library
Printed in Italy

CONTENTS

THE NEW TESTAMENT

FROM THE VERY BEGINNING OF TIME, God existed, everywhere, all-knowing, perfect. But the people He had created found it hard to understand the mind of God, because He was an invisible magnificence of spirit, not flesh and blood like us. For people to understand God better, He would have to send His son into the world to live a human life there, and teach people about goodness in words and by example. Even then, would they listen and understand?

From the very beginning of Time, God planned to send His son. That is why the Old Testament prophets spoke of a Messiah coming – a Saviour of God's Chosen People. The prophets knew that Jesus was coming. But they could never have expected the Jesus who arrived. The four Gospels of the New Testament tell the story not just of a Jew speaking to other Jews, but of the Son of God with a message for the whole world. The rest of the New Testament recounts how that message began to spread.

In the beginning was the Word, and the Word was with God, and the Word was God.
JOHN 1:1

And the Word was made flesh, and dwelt among us . . . full of grace and truth.
JOHN 1:14

THE BIRTH OF TWO BOYS

ZACHARIAS WAS A PRIEST. His days were spent among the cavernous arches and pillars, the sweet choking smell of incense, the whispered prayers of devout Jews, in the great Temple which was the heart of Jerusalem. As a priest, he could enter the holiest part of the Temple, hidden from the congregation by a curtain, to where an altar burned incandescent coals, and the ancient scrolls of scripture stood wrapped in rich cloth like motionless figures, waiting.

One day, from out of the smoke an angel appeared to Zacharias. "I have great news for you, Zacharias. Your wife Elisabeth will soon give birth to a baby boy."

Zacharias believed in visions - in angels, too - but not in such preposterous news as this. "All our lives we've wanted children! But no, no! It's not possible! We're both far too old!"

"You must call him John," the angel went on, as if Zacharias had not even spoken. "He will be a holy man with the power to make people listen. He will go on ahead, and tell the world of someone else who is coming. He'll prepare the way for a still greater man."

Bewildered and overcome by the sight he had seen, Zacharias stumbled out from behind the curtain of the Temple, making the people at their prayers look up and half rise from their knees. But when they asked him what was the matter, he spoke not a word in reply. He could not. Though his eyes were full of light, and his hands fluttered like wings, and his lips strained to sing with joy, he had no voice. The angel had taken it quite away.

Even when his wife Elisabeth told him the good news - that she was expecting a baby - he could only carve flourishes of joy on a tablet of wax, write down his delight in words.

Elisabeth had a cousin called Mary - a gentle, honest, kind girl

And there appeared unto him an angel of the Lord standing on the right side of the altar of incense.
LUKE 1:11

And when he came out, he could not speak unto them: and they perceived that he had seen a vision in the temple: for he beckoned unto them, and remained speechless.
LUKE 1:22

THE BIRTH OF
TWO BOYS

*And the angel came
in unto her, and
said, Hail, thou
that art highly
favoured, the Lord
is with thee: blessed
art thou among
women.*
LUKE 1:28

whom no one - not even her friends - could fault. She pleased God very much, as well. Mary was promised in marriage to Joseph the carpenter, but several weeks before the wedding, she received a visitor in the green shade of her parents' garden. Suddenly the birdsong fell silent and, in place of shadow, a pool of light fell over her. Dazzled, she looked up into the face of the Angel Gabriel.

"Greetings, Mary! Don't be afraid! I've come as God's messenger. A new life is about to begin in you. God has chosen to entrust to you His gift to the world. You shall be the mother of a baby - Jesus - Saviour of the World!"

"B-but how?" said Mary, trembling. "I'm not even married!"

"God who made the world will make the child in you," said the angel.

And Mary bowed her head and thanked God's messenger. For, though such a thing might bring down on her the scorn of her neighbours, God was surely honouring her more than any woman in all time. She was ready to do just as God wanted. Even if it cost her her marriage to Joseph.

When Joseph found out that Mary was expecting a baby, he was confused and shocked. He did not want the shame of marrying a woman who was already pregnant, whatever stories she might tell him of visiting angels and messages from God.

But that night, as Joseph slept, the Angel Gabriel stooped like an eagle into his dreams, crying, "Joseph! Don't break your promise to Mary! Don't think badly of her. The baby she is expecting is Jesus - Saviour of the World. Marry her just as you planned."

So Joseph married Mary and lived to be glad that he had.

Mary's cousin Elisabeth sensed, even as Mary came up the path towards the house, that there was something wonderful about the baby Mary was expecting.

"God has blessed us both, Mary. But most of all He has blessed you. Of all the women in the world He has chosen you to be the mother of His son. Ha ha! Feel! Here! The baby inside me is leaping and dancing, just because he's close to yours! From now till the end of time people are going to thank you for having this child!"

THE BIRTH OF TWO BOYS

And she shall bring forth a son, and thou shalt call his name Jesus: for he shall save his people from their sins.

MATTHEW 1:21

Blessed art thou among women, and blessed is the fruit of thy womb.

LUKE 1:42

THE BIRTH OF
TWO BOYS

*And he asked for a
writing table, and
wrote, saying, His
name is John.*

LUKE 1:63

Soon afterwards, Elisabeth's son was born, and naturally Zacharias's family and friends wanted to know: "What are you going to call him?" Zacharias still could not speak, so he wrote down his answer, carving the words in wax:

HIS NAME
IS
JOHN

At once, a rattling in his throat made him cough – and back came his voice. He could run to the window, to the roof, to the Temple steps and shout as loud as he liked, *"His name is John! His name is John! His name is John!"*

With such strange and wonderful events surrounding the birth of John, people began to wonder: could it be that *John* was the Saviour promised in the holy Scriptures? Many prophets had written about a "Messiah", a "Redeemer", coming to the rescue of God's Chosen People. And with Roman invaders occupying the country, surely now was as good a time as any for the rescuer to come? But prophecies are always couched in such poetic and mystical words. It was hard to be sure, hard to know for certain . . .

No. John was not the Messiah. He was only a messenger sent on ahead to prepare the way.

THE FIRST CHRISTMAS

A THOUSAND YEARS after King David, the kingdom he had ruled over was occupied by powerful
invaders - the Romans. Palestine was just one small corner of the
Roman Empire, its people the property of Emperor Caesar
Augustus, to do with as he liked. That year the Emperor ordered
everyone, wherever they were, to travel back to the place where
they had been born, so they could be counted and pay a poll tax
to the Roman government.

Mary and Joseph set off from their home, towards the town of
Bethlehem in Judaea, where Joseph's family came from. He was a
descendant (if a very remote and humble one) of the legendary
King David, and Bethlehem was where David himself had been
born. It was the city of the tribe of David. Mary rode on a donkey
while Joseph walked. It was a long, hard, jolting journey, made
worse by Mary's pregnancy: the baby was almost due.

*And it came to pass
in those days, that
there went out a
decree from Caesar
Augustus, that all
the world should
be taxed.*
LUKE 2:1

*And she brought
forth her firstborn
son, and wrapped
him in swaddling
clothes, and laid
him in a manger;
because there was
no room for them
in the inn.*
LUKE 2:7

*And there were in
the same country
shepherds abiding
in the field, keeping
watch over their
flock by night.
And, lo, the angel
of the Lord came
upon them . . .*
LUKE 2:8, 9

Bethlehem was crowded to overflowing, thanks to Caesar's decree. Every house and inn was already full by the time Joseph led his donkey into town. Its hooves clattered and slipped on paved roads. Crowds elbowed their way past. Joseph knocked at one door after another, but the answer was always the same: "No room! No room!" No room at any of the inns. Joseph leaned heavily on his staff. Mary groaned in the saddle. "No room! No room!"

At last one innkeeper took pity on the weary travellers. He must have seen that Mary was on the very point of having her baby. Or perhaps he saw how to make a few extra mites of money out of a pair of weary travellers. "There's no room indoors," he said, "but you can sleep in the stable, if you like."

So that is where Mary's baby was born - a dark, dirty, smelly place, the only warmth given off by the hairy flanks of cows, donkeys and horses, the only softness a sprinkling of straw. She called the child Jesus, and laid him in the animals' food-box, on a bed of straw. Joseph leaned over the crib to wonder at the miracle of new life, and the animals jostled restlessly in their stalls.

Not far away, a group of shepherds sat on a hillside looking after their sheep. They talked about the decree and all the traffic and upheaval it had caused. They dozed, ate and complained of the cold. They looked at the stars, as familiar a landscape to them as the daytime hills, and watched the orange haze of firelight fade from over the little town of Bethlehem, as the people there bedded down.

Suddenly a bright light made them sit up in terror. The sheep scattered, bleating. The shepherds reached out for their crooks and slingshots. "Look to the lambs!"

But no marauder was after the sheep. Above them in the sky, hovering like a hawk, as if on outspread wings of snow, a man of excelling beauty called out to them. "Don't be afraid!" he said. "I

am the Angel of the Lord God on High. I've come to bring you and everyone on Earth good news - marvellous news! A baby is being born, even now, in Bethlehem. His name is Jesus and he will save the world! Go and see for yourselves! You'll find him, using a manger for a cradle, in a stable by an inn. All Heaven is happy tonight!"

As he said it, a host of other angels came plunging through the starry sky, like silver dolphins leaping through a sea of black. They were shouting and singing, "Glory to God! Peace to His People on Earth!" Still singing and cheering, they soared upwards - higher and higher - until their brightness mingled with the galaxies.

The shepherds did not need to be told twice. "Let's go and see this baby! Let's go and see this marvellous thing that's happened!" And they left their sheep - left them! which goes against the nature of a shepherd - and walked down from the hills into Bethlehem and found the stable and the people sheltering inside it. Everything was just as the angels had said.

THE THREE WISE MEN

THE WORLD IS HUGE, but nestles in the vastness of one sky, just as it fits in the palm of God's hand. If God were to write a message - like Zacharias scratching on his wax tablet - where would He write it but on the night sky?

At around the time of Jesus's birth, a new star burst into being, bright enough to startle astronomers, strange enough to stir the imagination of astrologers. As the Earth rolled, so the star appeared to move - across the window of night - and in its wake came jingling bells - the bridle bells of camels and horses: a caravan moving westwards. Three seekers after Truth crossed many, many miles before they reached the kingdom of Judaea, on the fringes of the Roman Empire.

A local king ruled over Judaea in those days, holding power by permission of Caesar Augustus and the Roman authorities. He was called Herod. The three travellers presented themselves at Herod's palace: three wise philosophers, who read more in the stars than direction or season or myth. "We have come to see the new-born king," they explained, their eagerness thinly disguised by formal courtesies and greetings. "We saw a new star in the eastern sky, and our studies tell us that it signifies the birth of someone very important. As soon as we saw it, we left everything - didn't we, Melchior? - left our studies and our homes to follow the star. We just knew it would lead us to a mighty prince. Is he here? Do you know where we can find him? We must pay tribute to him!"

"A new king born?" thought Herod. "*I* am the only king hereabouts! And after me my son will be the only king. I must find this newborn, so-called 'king' and kill him before he is old enough to steal my crown from me! No one calls themselves 'king' in *my* domain!"

Now when Jesus was born in Bethlehem of Judaea in the days of Herod the king, behold, there came wise men from the east to Jerusalem, Saying, Where is he that is born King of the Jews?
MATTHEW 2:1, 2

But he said none of this to the three travellers, plucking his lower lip between finger and thumb, stroking the plush of his robe. All that showed on his face was a happy curiosity - a lively interest in the philosophers' startling news. "The baby isn't here. I don't know where he is. But when the star has led you to him, do *please* come back and tell me, won't you? So that I can go and . . . *pay tribute* too." and he smiled unctuously, as if the thought of a new-born baby filled him with sentimental joy.

The three philosophers promised to do so and went on their way. It was true, the star was not poised, strictly speaking, directly over the palace, now that they looked more carefully. It stood, more precisely, over Bethlehem. In fact, when they reached Bethlehem, the star seemed to glimmer high above a stable - directly over its roof - but what would a mighty, newborn

prince be doing in the stable of an inn? The three philosophers went in.

Despite the shabby surroundings, despite the very *ordinary* appearance of the man and woman and baby sheltering there, the wise men knelt down in front of the manger and presented gifts fit for a king.

The first philosopher gave gold, because Jesus was to be the king of all kings.

The second gave frankincense - the fragrance burned in holy places - because Jesus was someone sent from the realms of Heaven.

The third gave myrrh - used to perfume dead bodies before they were buried. Perhaps he knew Jesus would die all too soon.

Mary thanked them, but kept her innermost thoughts to herself, and treasured in her heart the memory of that strange visit.

THE THREE
WISE MEN

And when they were come into the house, they saw the young child with Mary his mother, and fell down, and worshipped him: and when they had opened their treasures, they presented unto him gifts; gold, and frankincense, and myrrh.
MATTHEW 2:11

*And being warned
of God in a dream
that they should not
return to Herod,
they departed into
their own country
another way.*
MATTHEW 2:12

As the three wise men slept that night, an angel flew into their dreams, like a bird restless to migrate. "Don't go back to King Herod," he said. "Don't tell him where you found Jesus. Of all the people in the world, you mustn't tell Herod."

When they woke, they compared dreams. Quickly they saddled their camels and hurried homewards, leaving the country by a different route.

When the three wise pilgrims did not report back, Herod refused to be thwarted. He would find out all he could about the "newborn king." He sent for his holy men and advisers, and demanded to know what they could tell him. The scholars searched the holy Scriptures like ants in a granary, until they came to a passage talking about Bethlehem, the city of David. It seemed to be saying that a great saviour would be born there one day.

"Bethlehem? *Bethlehem*?" raged Herod. *"So what are you waiting for? Kill all the baby boys in Bethlehem!"*

With his soldiers on their way to carry out this terrible command,

Herod thought gleefully that he was rid of his rival once and for all. But God's plans are not so easily scotched, nor are angels hampered by distance or by night.

An angel flew through Joseph's dreams that night, like a swan fleeing from a hunter's arrows. "Wake up, Joseph!" he said. "You and your wife and the baby Jesus are in terrible danger. Leave Bethlehem. Leave Judaea! Run for Egypt, and hide there until the danger is past!"

So the little family fled into Egypt and Herod's murdering soldiers found no one in the stable of that inn in Bethlehem, though they turned over the straw with their swords and chased the cattle out into the street.

To and fro, to and fro sped the angels of the Lord on many, many missions. But it was not until many months had passed that Joseph's dreams were once again feathered with angels, and God sent word that Herod was dead. Joseph and Mary were safe to go home to Judaea. They settled in a new place - in the town of Nazareth. And that is where Jesus grew up and spent most of his life.

And when they were departed, behold, the angel of the Lord appeareth to Joseph in a dream, saying, Arise, and take the young child and his mother, and flee into Egypt, and be thou there until I bring thee word: for Herod will seek the young child to destroy him.
MATTHEW 2:13

THANK YOU FOR JESUS

IN THOSE DAYS, the parents of a baby boy used to show how grateful they were to God by taking their son to the great Temple in Jerusalem and offering up a sacrifice of two turtledoves. So as soon as they were able, Mary and Joseph took Jesus to the Temple to say thank you.

There were two very religious people living in Jerusalem just then; one old priest called Simeon and an old lady - a prophetess called Anna. She never actually left the Temple, but had made it her home so that she could worship God night and day. Simeon had been promised that he would not die until he had seen the Messiah, the Saviour foretold in the holy Scriptures.

But a man can only live so long. He gets tired, disheartened, begins to doubt things of which he was once certain. So it was that Simeon sat dozing, his knobbly hands folded in his lap, his head drooping, when into the bright rectangle of the Temple doorway stepped two figures: a man and a young woman holding a child in her arms.

Simeon stumbled to his feet. He snatched Jesus out of Mary's arms and swung him up high so that the little boy laughed. "Oh! Now I am content to die, Lord!" cried Simeon. "I have seen the Saviour of the World with my own eyes!" Mary and Joseph were amazed, but when Simeon turned to them his smile was tempered by sadness. "This child will be the making and undoing of many people in Israel," he told them. "And there will be some who say evil things about him. Your heart will be broken, too," he told Mary.

Simeon's shout still rang in the Temple eaves. Anna had heard it and came over, attracted by curiosity. She saw him in an instant - the answer to all her prayers. And taking the baby out of Simeon's

Lord, now lettest thou thy servant depart in peace, according to thy word: For mine eyes have seen thy salvation, Which thou hast prepared before the face of all people . . .
LUKE 2:29, 30, 31

arms she danced with him, round and round, making a most outrageous and unseemly noise as she shouted her thanks into the rafters. "Oh Lord God, you sent him! You sent him before I died! Oh thank you! Thank you, thank you!"

Joseph shuffled his feet and looked around, embarrassed. Mary smiled a secret, wistful smile, and waited patiently for Anna to bring back her baby boy. From that day onward old Anna could be seen in and around the Temple telling everyone she met about the boy Jesus, God's gift to the world.

THANK YOU
FOR JESUS

And she coming in that instant gave thanks likewise unto the Lord, and spake of him to all them that looked for redemption in Jerusalem.
LUKE 2:38

. . . after three days they found him in the temple, sitting in the midst of the doctors, both hearing them, and asking them questions. And all that heard him were astonished at his understanding and answers.
LUKE 2:46, 47

Of course by the time Jesus was twelve, both Anna and Simeon were long gone from the Temple precincts. Though once a year Mary, Joseph and Jesus would travel to Jerusalem to celebrate the festival of Passover, they were never again greeted with such excitement.

They would travel in among a big group of friends and relations, meeting other pilgrims along the way. At the end of the festivities, the prayers, the singing, the long journey home to Nazareth began. Countless people milled and jostled along the road - such a clamour of camels grunting, pots clattering, children laughing. It was easy to lose sight of someone in a crowd like that. Mary and Joseph supposed that twelve-year-old Jesus must be playing with other boys somewhere within the clattering caravan. A whole day passed before they realized Jesus was not with the party at all. Nobody had seen him, not since leaving Jerusalem!

Distraught, panic-stricken, the parents turned back, imagining dreadful accidents, terrible troubles overtaking their dear son. Re-entering Jerusalem, they searched and searched the city, growing more and more frantic by the hour. At last, after three nightmarish days, they decided to try one last place - the Temple. They had been there with Jesus, and even if he had not been left behind, lost among the towering columns or asleep in one of the little dark recesses, they could at least pray to God for help to find their missing son.

And there he was! In the Temple! He was sitting among the grown men: the scholars, philosophers and rabbis, listening to them and asking remarkably sensible questions. In fact the men he was with could hardly believe they were talking with a boy of only twelve.

In her astonishment and relief, Mary began to tell Jesus off in no uncertain terms. "How could you! We've been so worried! We've looked everywhere!"

But Jesus seemed surprised. "Didn't you know I would be here? Didn't you know I'd be doing the things my Father sent me to do?'

It is hard for parents to feel put in their place by their own child. Joseph might have flown into a rage. But though, at the time, Mary and Joseph did not understand, still they knew enough to keep silent. After many years, no doubt, things would become plain. In the meantime, of course, Jesus had to go back with them to Nazareth, like a good, obedient son. There he grew into a strong, sensible, devout young man - a credit, you might say, to his Father.

And he said unto them, How is it that ye sought me? wist ye not that I must be about my Father's business?

LUKE 2:49

JOHN THE BAPTIST

In those days came John the Baptist, preaching in the wilderness of Judaea, And saying, Repent ye: for the kingdom of heaven is at hand.

MATTHEW 3:1, 2

AS JESUS GREW UP, so, of course, did the son of Zacharias and Elisabeth. His name, you will remember, was John, and he came to be called "John the Baptist" because he made it his job to convert people, to wring repentance from them and then sink them in the holy River Jordan to wash away their sins and make them right with God.

He did not preach in the towns, but in wild, desert places, where he lived by eating locusts as well as honey from the hives of wild bees. He must have looked very wild himself, dishevelled and ill-fed, in a coarse camel-hair tunic. Still, people from all quarters came trekking to hear him.

The message he had for them was urgent and fierce: "Now is your very last chance! Be sorry for your sins and begin a new life; God's Kingdom will soon be here - down *here* on Earth!" His words had a quality which pierced to the very heart, and whole families, whole crowds of families begged forgiveness for wrongs they had done in the past, wanting to make a fresh start. Then John would baptize them in the River Jordan, pushing them under the water, lifting them out again - to show they were washed clean of past mistakes.

John had no patience with the priests and so-called holy men down in the city synagogues and temples. When they came to watch him preach, he minced no words in saying just what he thought of them: "Think yourselves better than ordinary men, don't you? Well, some of you are much worse!" It did not make him popular.

Of course there were people who still mistook John for the Messiah promised in the holy Scriptures, but he told the crowds plainly, "I baptize you with river water, but there is someone

I indeed baptize you with water unto repentance: but he that cometh after me is mightier than I . . . he shall baptize you with the Holy Ghost, and with fire . . .
MATTHEW 3:11

And lo a voice from heaven, saying, This is my beloved Son, in whom I am well pleased.
MATTHEW 3:17

coming who will baptize you with fire! You think I'm a holy man? I won't be worthy even to fasten his sandals!"

Then, one day, Jesus himself was among the crowd.

John straightened up from submerging a convert in the muddy water and there stood his cousin, watching the river, watching John. In fact he was coming down towards the river, even now, dropping his robe on the bank, for all the world as if he wanted to be baptized like all the others. John plunged forward to meet Jesus, hampered by the water round his thighs. Their hands met. "It's *you* who should be baptizing *me*, not the other way round!" John protested.

But Jesus said quietly, "Just let it be like this for now."

So John baptized Jesus in the River Jordan, and as Jesus waded out of the water afterwards, hair streaming, water glittering on his lashes, it was almost as if the sky was torn open. The stillness of the day was pierced by an unusually penetrating light. Something as gentle and tender as a dove settled on Jesus where he stood knotting the belt once more around his pale robe. And a voice called from nowhere, from out of the sky, from everywhere: "This is my own dear son. I am *very* pleased with him."

Not long afterwards, John the Baptist was arrested by the authorities. "A trouble-maker," they said. "A rabble-rouser. Put him in prison and throw away the key. Let us hear no more from this 'baptizing' preacher. His kind are nothing but trouble."

FORTY DAYS IN THE WILDERNESS

To prepare himself for his great task of teaching and preaching, Jesus, at the age of thirty, went out into the desert, just as John had done. He spent forty days and forty nights there, denying himself food or shelter, depriving his body of comfort so as to enrich that other more important part of him: his soul.

Towards the end of the forty days, he was famished, parched, dizzy. The desert melted into mirages; the sky puddled into patches of dark. The blood sang in his ears, and sleep blurred with wakefulness.

And then there came visions. It seemed as if the Devil himself – the same Tempter, perhaps, who had tricked Adam and Eve in the Garden of Eden – came to Jesus and tempted him to turn his back on God. In such a place, after such a fast, it was enough to test anybody's strength and goodness to breaking point.

"If you really are the Son of God, why don't you turn the stones into bread?" Already they looked like loaves, those brown

And when the Tempter came to him, he said, If thou be the Son of God, command that these stones be made bread. But he answered and said, It is written, Man shall not live by bread alone, but by every word that proceedeth out of the mouth of God.
Matthew 4:3, 4

rocks flour-dusty with sand. In this oven of a desert, the very air seemed to smell of baking bread.

But hungry as he was, Jesus could wrestle with temptation. "Don't you read the Scriptures? None of us keeps alive just by eating bread; we need the word of God to feed our souls, too." He shut his eyes against the sun-baked wilderness.

When he opened them again, he reeled dizzily. For it seemed that he was balancing on the very topmost pinnacle of the great Temple in Jerusalem. The whole city lay spread out at his feet.

"If you were really the Son of God, you could throw yourself down from here and not suffer so much as a scratch. Doesn't it

say in the Scriptures that the angels will watch over you and take care that you never so much as stub your foot on a stone? Think what a stir that would cause! Besides, then you'd know – once and for all – for absolutely certain, no dregs of doubt left . . . that you really are the Messiah. How else can you be sure? Do it! Jump! Jump down and live!"

But Jesus closed his eyes against the dizzying, glorious view. Perhaps he could resist the glory, for any street magician can win gasps of admiration. But the certainty of knowing, the end to all self-doubt, that must have smelled very sweet indeed. Jesus looked the Tempter in the eye. "It also says in the Scriptures,

FORTY DAYS IN
THE WILDERNESS

*Jesus said unto
him, It is written
again, Thou shalt
not tempt the Lord
thy God.*
MATTHEW 4:7

*Then saith Jesus
unto him, Get thee
hence, Satan: for it
is written, Thou
shalt worship the
Lord thy God,
and him only shalt
thou serve.*
Matthew 4:10

'Don't set tests for God, to see if He can pass them.' "

It did not spare him further torment. Suddenly, it seemed to Jesus that he had been lifted higher still, and was standing on the peak of the highest mountain in the world, while the Tempter showed him, like some fawning tailor unrolling bolts of cloth, all the kingdoms of the world spread out below.

"Trust me. Trust! I will make you ruler over all this - over the entire world . . . if you'll just admit: it's all mine really - all of my making, all intended to glorify Satan. Worship me and I tell you, it's yours."

Gasping for breath in the thin, rarefied air, Jesus turned angrily on his sly, grinning persecutor: "Get behind me, Satan! Take yourself off! I shall do what the Scriptures tell me to do and worship God and God alone."

And suddenly peace returned to the thorny wilderness. The temptations were over. The Tempter had failed, and left Jesus alone . . . for the time being, at least.

JESUS GATHERS HIS FOLLOWERS

IT WAS TIME FOR JESUS to begin work. After John the Baptist had been put into prison, Jesus left Nazareth and went down to the Sea of Galilee - to Capernaum - and began to preach and say (just as John had done), "Now is the time to be sorry for your sins, because God's Kingdom will soon be here on Earth!"

One day, Jesus was walking by the great lake of Galilee, when he saw two brothers, both fishermen, Simon (who was later called Peter) and Andrew, fishing close in to the shore. "Come with me and I'll have you catching people's souls instead of fish!"

Without question, without a second thought, the two brothers left their nets. They did not stop to wonder where their next meal would come from, or what dangers they might face in joining up with an outspoken radical like Jesus. They simply chose to be his disciples, his followers, and to travel with him on his journeys and learn all he had to teach them.

Next, Jesus saw two other brothers, James and John, fishing with their father Zebedee. He called out to them too to come and share his work. Immediately they left their lives as fishermen and followed him. Something about this man was so inspiring that ordinary men with jobs to do and families to feed were ready to drop everything and go who knows where, regardless of the outcome.

In due course, Jesus chose other disciples - twelve in all - from among the people that came to hear him preach. There was Philip and Bartholomew, Matthew and Thomas, another James and Thaddaeus, another Simon and lastly Judas Iscariot. It is interesting, that name - Iscariot. It means "dagger-carrier". Before Judas joined Jesus he was a member of a group of freedom fighters dedicated to driving out the Roman armies of occupation. The dagger-carriers

And he saith unto them, Follow me, and I will make you fishers of men.
MATTHEW 4:19

did not much care how it was achieved: a knife between the ribs of a Roman guard, a cord round the throat of a Roman official, or full-scale rebellion. Many Jews supposed that the promised Messiah would do just that - head an uprising to drive out the Romans, and establish a free Jewish state. Perhaps Judas Iscariot thought that was what Jesus meant to do, and that is why he joined him. But why did Jesus choose Judas, that odd man out, that violent, angry young man? Perhaps he knew, from the very start, what role Judas would play in the drama, and chose him to play out his part to the bitter end.

Jesus renamed one of his followers. He told Simon, "I shall call you Peter, which means 'a rock'. I need someone sure and solid and reliable I can depend on - a foundation I can build on."

Jesus, with his twelve disciples, travelled about the country teaching in the synagogues where people worshipped, and in the open air. He had a genius for telling stories, a way with words - a way with people, too. Jesus was popular, no doubt about it, and his disciples probably had no doubts, in those early days, that they had made the right decision, thrown in their lot with the man of the moment.

And I say also unto thee, That thou art Peter, and upon this rock I will build my church; and the gates of hell shall not prevail against it.

MATTHEW 16:18

WATER INTO WINE

IT WAS SOMEBODY'S WEDDING DAY in Cana: a day to down tools and put on clean clothes, to join the noisy guests celebrating in the street and to dance with them all the way from the synagogue, through the town and home to the bridegroom's house for a party! Everyone was invited: friends, relations, passersby, and since Jesus and his disciples were in town, visiting Mary and the rest of the family, naturally they were included in the invitation. Everyone is welcome at a wedding - the more the merrier!

Unfortunately, guests drink wine, and the bridegroom had not ordered enough; it ran out before the end of the feast. The servants were in a real panic. No wine at a wedding? Calamity! They told Mary, and Mary told Jesus. Then she turned to the servants and said, "Do whatever my son tells you."

Standing by the door of the house were six big stone jars intended to hold water. Jesus told the servants, "Fill up the jars at the well. Then be quick and serve the bride's father; his glass is empty."

They did just as they were told, though it seemed monumentally risky. Serve the father of the bride - *the most important guest* - with a cup of water? They filled the jars at the well, then carried one to the table where the guests were waiting (none too patiently) for a drink. When the jug was upended, the liquid inside came bubbling out . . .

Fortunately, the bride's father knew nothing about the awful matter of the wine shortage. He took one sip and called out to the bridegroom, "Well! Most weddings I've been to, people serve the best wine at the beginning and bring out the cheap stuff when everyone's too drunk to tell the difference! You, you've saved the best till last!"

When the ruler of the feast had tasted the water that was made wine, and knew not whence it was: (but the servants which drew the water knew;) the governor of the feast called the bridegroom, And saith unto him, Every man at the beginning doth set forth good wine; and when men have well drunk, then that which is worse: but thou hast kept the good wine until now.

JOHN 2:9, 10

Everyone was delighted and, six stone jars later, probably rather sleepy as well. The watching disciples, of course, looked at Jesus with a new kind of admiration: like children watching magic. But Jesus was no magician; he was a worker of miracles. And miracles are about more than party tricks or granting wishes. Miracles are about transforming *people* and the whole of their lives. Jesus took people weak as water and made them strong as heady liquor, filled them to the brim with joy. That was the real magic.

RAGE IN THE TEMPLE

WHEN THE YEARLY FEAST of Passover came round, Jesus and his friends went up to Jerusalem to celebrate it - just as they had when they were children hand in hand with their parents. Naturally, Jesus went to the Temple to pray.

Over the years, a practice had grown up of market traders setting up their stalls *inside* the courtyards of the Temple. There were birdcages rattling with doves and pigeons, pens heaving with oxen, folds filled with sheep. These were the animals for sale to worshippers who wanted to make a burnt sacrifice to God. Consequently, the air was noisy with clucking, mooing and bleating, the shriek of animals being slaughtered, the shouts of animal-sellers recommending their particular beasts as best. Flies mustered around the blood. The Temple yard looked half farmyard, half abattoir. There were cash desks, too, where the money-changers hunched over their piles of coins, their fingers black with counting small change. Worshippers were expected to pay a tribute of money into the Temple offertory boxes, but it was considered unholy to offer the Roman coins used for everyday buying and selling. So the money-changers in the Temple yard would exchange the Roman coins for Jewish ones - and make a tidy profit doing it.

When Jesus saw what an unholy market-place the Temple had become, he was gripped by a violent rage. He made up a whip with several cord lashes, and raged through the yards overturning stalls, opening birdcages and driving the traders out of the Temple gates. "You've made my Father's house into a den of thieves!" he stormed.

If Jesus's disciples were taken aback, the Jews in and around the Temple, the loosed doves battering in their faces, were

And when he had made a scourge of small cords, he drove them all out of the temple, and the sheep, and the oxen; and poured out the changers' money, and overthrew the tables . . .
JOHN 2: 15

outraged. "How dare you! What are you, God's own man? What gives you the right to go breaking up the place? You're nothing but a trouble-maker! Who gave you the right to come wrecking our trade? God, you say? Let's see it, then! Where's the proof God sent you?"

"There will be proof," said Jesus mysteriously. "Destroy this Temple and I will build it again in three days."

"Oh yes?" scoffed the Jews. "Years this Temple took to build, and you'll build it again in three days, will you?"

But Jesus was not talking about *their* Temple, the one built out of stone and brick. Nobody understood him then, and the words were to make terrible trouble for him. But truly he was talking about his *own body*. If the Jews destroyed *that* temple - killed him, buried him, snuffed him out entirely - still he would be back in three days.

And he was.

What better proof could there be that Jesus was God's own man?

Jesus answered and said unto them, Destroy this temple, and in three days I will raise it up.
JOHN 2:19

BORN AGAIN

THE PHARISEES were the highest officials in the Jewish religion. They were powerful men who controlled the spiritual life of every religious Jew. Unfortunately, their power had made them smug and narrow-minded, and they did not like anything or anyone to upset their comfortable lives, to question their ideas and customs. Oh, they knew off by heart all the complicated rules and laws of their religion - and kept them, too - but they had rather forgotten that the rules and laws were just guidelines meant to help them love God and care for each other. Most of the Pharisees *hated* Jesus. The people flocked into the countryside to hang on his every word, instead of listening obediently at the feet of the Pharisees. He was a threat to their influence and easy existence.

Nicodemus was rather different. He was a Pharisee. But he had heard a little of what Jesus had to say, and he wanted to hear more. Nervous of being seen by someone who might recognize him, Nicodemus came to visit Jesus at night. He said, "Teacher, I've seen the miracles you perform. No one can do such things unless he has the power of God in him. Tell me what I must do to please God!"

Jesus said, "Unless a person is born again, it is impossible for him to please God, or become a member of God's family."

Nicodemus was completely baffled. "Born again? How can anyone do that? A grown man can't climb back into his mother's womb, can he, and be born again?"

"Ah, but I'm not talking about a person's physical body," said Jesus. "I'm talking about his *soul*. Our bodies are born out of our parents, yes. But our souls are born out of the Holy Spirit - and the Holy Spirit is like the wind - you can't see where it comes from or where it goes, but everyone knows it's there. It's a person's

Jesus answered, Verily, verily, I say unto thee, Except a man be born of water and of the Spirit, he cannot enter into the Kingdom of God. That which is born of the flesh is flesh; and that which is born of the Spirit is spirit.
JOHN 3:5, 6

For God so loved the world, that he gave his only begotten Son, that whosoever believeth in him should not perish, but have everlasting life. For God sent not his Son into the world to condemn the world; but that the world through him might be saved.

JOHN 3:16, 17

soul that is reborn when he or she makes the decision to accept God's love and start living in a new way, a better way."

Nicodemus tugged at his beard, still struggling with the difficulty of the idea. Jesus was dismayed: "Don't *you* understand - you who are supposed to be among the wisest and best men in the whole nation?"

Even so, Nicodemus could not have been such a poor student, because it was in him that Jesus chose to confide the most marvellous truth of all. "God loved the world so much," he said, "that He sent His only son into it to give people the chance of believing and of living for ever and ever. It's all a matter of believing, Nicodemus. Those who believe will be saved and those who don't believe will be lost. Some people prefer to live in the dark where their wickedness can't be seen. So they hate the light when it shows them up for what they are. That's why some won't be glad to see God's son coming in their direction . . . But God didn't send His son to condemn people - just to offer them a way of making everything right again with God."

Nicodemus nodded and, rapt in thought, turned for the door. As he opened it, he was confronted by the blackness of the unlit street outside. But light from the doorway spilled out around and ahead of him, like a pathway into the dark. He stepped out boldly into the night.

A PROPHET IN HIS OWN COUNTRY

IN HIS OWN TOWN OF NAZARETH, too, Jesus went to the synagogue on the Sabbath and read the set passage of scripture for the day. The words he read were those of a prophet foretelling the coming of the Messiah. They spoke of someone coming ". . . to preach the good news to the poor . . . to comfort the brokenhearted, to tell prisoners that they are free, to give sight to the blind . . ."

At the end of the reading, Jesus closed the book, gave it back to the priest and sat down. The eyes of everyone in the synagogue were on him, waiting for him to talk about the passage he had just read. He said, "Today that prophecy I read out to you has come true."

What a stir that caused! "What's that? What did he say? What does he mean? That *he's* the Messiah? Isn't this the Jesus we've all known since he was a boy? The son of Joseph the carpenter?"

Jesus did not try to argue with them. "Perhaps you've heard rumours about me. You'll be saying to yourselves, 'Let's see him work wonders here.' But what would be the point if I did? A prophet is never respected or believed in his own country. Nobody can ever credit there is anything remarkable about someone they have lived alongside for years."

This did not please the people of Nazareth. They fumed and curled their lips. They hustled Jesus out of the synagogue, out of the city itself and jostled him to the top of a high bluff, meaning to throw him off it, meaning to murder him for his insults and for giving himself such airs.

But the very strength of his character, the very power of his personality was too great for them. Like the Red Sea before Moses, the mob parted. Calm and unruffled, Jesus walked away from the

The Spirit of the Lord is upon me, because he hath anointed me to preach the gospel to the poor; he hath sent me to heal the brokenhearted, to preach deliverance to the captives, and recovering of sight to the blind, to set at liberty them that are bruised.
LUKE 4:18

And he said, Verily I say unto you, No prophet is accepted in his own country.
LUKE 4:24

precipice, and passed right through the crowd. Not a man dared so much as to lay a finger on him.

But he left Nazareth after that and went back to Capernaum to teach there instead, where people took notice of what he said, and were more ready to take it to heart. But it must have been hard, to face such stony resentment and disbelief in the faces of people he knew, neighbours he had grown up with; even his own relations.

THE WOMAN BY THE WELL

THE JOURNEYS OF JESUS and his disciples took them through Samaria. Now the Jews in those days looked down on the people of Samaria as if they were some lower form of life altogether - would never so much as speak to one, since Samaritans chose to worship God on a holy mountain, while Jews said the Temple in Jerusalem was the only proper place.

Even though it was early morning, the air was hot, the land dry and dusty, with little patches of vivid green where irrigation had watered a bite of grass for the cattle, a plot of vegetables. Around the village well, green trees deeply rooted cast a merciful shade, and already many footprints overlapped on the dusty ground, where village women had come and gone, tall waterpots balanced on their heads.

While his disciples were away buying food, Jesus sat on the edge of Jacob's well. It was early morning, and the women of the town were coming to fetch water, letting down their buckets on a rope. "Would you give me some water, please?" said Jesus.

The woman was startled. "A Jew asking a Samaritan for water?"

"Ah, we Jews have always claimed to know God better than you Samaritans, haven't we? But soon it won't matter if people worship on a mountain or in a Temple, so long as they worship God in their hearts. That's all God cares about. The news I've brought is for everyone everywhere, not just the Jews."

As the woman took a sip of water she had drawn, Jesus said "I can give you a different kind of water to drink . . ."

"What do you mean, you could give me water? Where's your bucket?"

Jesus went on, "Anyone who drinks this well-water will get thirsty again in time and need another drink. But the kind of

But whosoever drinketh of the water that I shall give him shall never thirst; but the water that I shall give him shall be in him a well of water springing up into everlasting life.
JOHN 4:14

*Jesus saith unto
her, I that speak
unto thee am he.*
JOHN 4:26

water I can give you would quench your thirst everlastingly."

"Give me some then!" laughed the woman. "I'll never need to carry heavy buckets to and fro again!"

"I'm talking about the thirst in your soul - the thirst to know about God and how to put yourself right with God. Fetch your husband, why don't you, and I'll tell you both my news."

"I haven't got a husband," said the woman.

"I'm glad you admit it," said Jesus. "I know that the man you're living with isn't your husband - nor were the five men you lived with before that."

The woman was flabbergasted to hear that this total stranger knew all her secrets. "You know everything about me! You must be a prophet!" Jesus asked her what she knew about God and the Scriptures. "I know there is a Messiah coming who will be the saving of us all - Jew and Samaritan."

And Jesus said, "I am that Messiah."

Just then, the disciples came back and were amazed to see Jesus deep in conversation with a *Samaritan* woman. The woman went back into the town and rushed about telling everyone, "The Messiah has come! He's sitting by the well, and he knew everything about me although he's never met me before! Go and see! Go and see!"

They went out of curiosity, to see (they supposed) some kind of fortune-teller. But when they had sat and listened to Jesus, they came back into the town and told her, "We went to take a look at him because he knew all about you; we stayed and listened because of what he said to us. You were right. He *is* the Messiah!"

So Jesus gave the despised people of Samaria a drink of water - the kind that quenched the thirst in their souls.

When his disciples pressed him to eat the food they had bought, he said something similar: "I have another food to keep me going. I have God's Word to feed my soul. That's the most important hunger to satisfy."

HEALING MIND AND BODY

IN THOSE DAYS, people thought of illness as a punishment. For a person to be ill, they must have done something wrong. Mental illness and such baffling, frightening disorders as epilepsy were considered the work of devils: evil spirits invading a person's body and taking possession of it. Even the people who were sick would have believed this, believed themselves possessed by demons.

One day, when Jesus was preaching in the synagogue in Capernaum, a poor deranged man starting ranting and shouting out, "Leave me alone, Jesus of Nazareth! Leave me in peace! I know you! You've come to destroy me! I know you: you're God's holy messenger!" Everyone there took it to be not the man talking, but the evil spirit inside him.

So Jesus said, as if to the evil spirit, "Be quiet and come out!"

The man fell into a terrible, racking fit which flung him about like a rag doll in the jaws of a dog. It looked as though the demon inside him was resisting with tooth and claw being dragged forcibly out into the glare of daylight. People stepped aside, drawing their hands in against their chests, looking away in distaste, or staring in horrid fascination. But Jesus stepped closer, crouched down, held the man's thrashing head.

And Jesus rebuked him, saying, Hold thy peace, and come out of him. And when the unclean spirit had torn him, and cried with a loud voice, he came out of him.
MARK 1:25, 26

*And he came and
took her by the
hand, and lifted her
up; and immediately
the fever left her,
and she ministered
unto them.*

MARK 1:31

When the fit was over, the man sat up, as calm and sane and untroubled as the next man. The congregation was amazed. "What is this we're seeing? What kind of rabbi is this? Even evil spirits do as he tells them!" They scarcely knew whether to be pleased or suspicious. After all, someone who is more powerful than a demon is also more alarming.

After he left the synagogue that day, Jesus went to stay at the home of his friends Simon and Andrew. They must have been anxious to tell the family what had happened at the synagogue - about the healing, about the joy of the miracle of a man set free from his demons. But their joy turned to sudden sadness and anxiety. They found the house a silent, sorry place. Simon's mother-in-law was ill: everyone was afraid for her life. Jesus went straight to her bedside and held her frail hand all sweaty with fever.

At once her temperature dropped.

In fact the fever lifted, like fog in the sunshine, and the old lady woke feeling perfectly well. She sat up, snatched her hand back abruptly from Jesus and looked around her with a disapproving scowl. "What's all this standing about? What a fuss and a flurry. Don't you know I've got a dinner to cook? Well, look lively, Andrew! Fetch me my sandals. There are visitors in the house, lad! The dinner won't cook itself!"

News like that gets about. People came from all over town, even after sunset, bringing sick relations and friends. The whole city seemed to have gathered outside the door. Words of wisdom are one thing, but the gift of good health is beyond price. Anyone who has been desperately ill, or seen someone they love suffer serious sickness understands the inexpressible value of a cure, a healer, an end to illness.

Many went home to bed that night healed in body and mind who had been sick and troubled before.

Next morning, long before dawn, Jesus got up and found himself a quiet, deserted place to pray. Simon and the others came to find him: "Everyone is looking for you. They want more miracles."

"Then let's move on," said Jesus, "so that I can teach. That's what I came to do first and foremost."

He travelled right through Galilee preaching . . . and of course healing people, too, because wherever he went, unhappy people pleaded for his help.

One day it was a leper, his skin snowy white with disease. Leprosy so frightened people then that they drove lepers away to live as outcasts, forebade them to come near healthy people, called them "unclean". Nothing remained then but a life of begging and loneliness, while the disease ate away at the body and despair ate away at the soul. This leper threw himself down at Jesus's feet and begged, "Make me clean! You can if you want, I know it!"

Jesus felt such a wealth of pity for the man that he put out his

HEALING MIND
AND BODY

And there came a leper to him, beseeching him, and kneeling down to him, and saying unto him, If thou wilt, thou canst make me clean. And Jesus, moved with compassion, put forth his hand, and touched him, and saith unto him, I will; be thou clean.

MARK 1:40, 41

And when they could not come nigh unto him for the press, they uncovered the roof where he was: and when they had broken it up, they let down the bed wherein the sick of the palsy lay.
MARK 2:4

hand and touched him - touched a leper, imagine! "I do want it," he said. "Be well." At once, the skin lost its patchy whiteness; feeling came back into numb fingers and toes. The man was no longer that despised, dying creature, a "leper"; he was a person again. "Don't tell anyone what has happened to you," said Jesus. "Just go and show yourself to the priest to prove you are well enough to go home. Thank God - and keep this a secret between us."

What a hope! The man was so overjoyed that he told everyone he met, "Jesus of Nazareth made me well! The great teacher made me well! Look at me! I'm well! I'm well!"

The result was, of course, that Jesus could not go near a city without being mobbed. He had to stay outside, in the countryside and desert, and people came out from the towns to find him and hear him teach. They came from *everywhere*. When he risked a night's rest in Capernaum, word got out, and people packed the house to the very doors. Even some Pharisees had come along to see this celebrated healer and what he could do. There was no room to move, let alone for latecomers to squeeze their way through to Jesus.

So the four men who had brought their friend on a stretcher could not get anywhere near Jesus to ask for his help. The man on the bed was paralysed. He was lucky to have such friends, for the world can be very cruel to a man who cannot walk.

When the four saw the crowd, they went to the side of the house instead, where a stone staircase led up to the flat roof. And once up on the roof, they took it to pieces tile by tile. Through the gaping hole they lowered down the stretcher on four ropes.

Swinging down towards Jesus's head came the sad sight of the paralysed man. Jesus was deeply moved by the efforts of the friends and by the man's faith that he could be healed. He looked the man in the eye and said, "Your sins are forgiven."

Not the words of a doctor. The Pharisees muttered and scowled. "What does he mean, 'sins forgiven'? Only God can forgive sins!"

*I say unto thee,
Arise, and take up
thy bed, and go thy
way into thine
house.*

MARK 2:11

Jesus of course sensed what they were saying. "What do you think will do this man more good: to hear that his body is healed, or that his sins are forgiven? . . . But since you want proof of forgiveness . . ." He turned back to the paralysed man: "Pick up your bed and walk."

Immediately the man got up, folded the stretcher and walked out of the house - careful little steps at first, then long strides and finally great bounding leaps of joy, as if he might jump over the moon.

KEEPING BAD COMPANY

SOME DAYS JESUS sat down to dinner with a motley crowd - rogues, ne'er-do-wells, less-than-respectable women and some of that hated breed, the tax-collector. Tax-collectors were Jews who worked for the occupying Roman government, collecting taxes from their own people and being bitterly resented for it too. But one of Jesus's own disciples was an ex-tax-collector. Jesus did not despise anyone. When the Pharisees saw the kind of company Jesus was keeping, they shook their heads grimly and tut-tutted. "Look at him," they said, "eating with tax-collectors and sinners!"

Jesus looked up, "Who else *would* I spend my time with? Where's the point in telling *good* people how to be good? That's like curing people who aren't ill! Doctors are for curing the sick. I came to teach people who have gone wrong how to start afresh. That's why I'm here - for the sinners, not the saints."

Still the Pharisees carped and complained. "John the Baptist used to fast - to go without food for days on end. Why don't your disciples fast? It's what *religious* people do. Why don't they?"

Jesus looked around fondly at his disciples as they sat about in the sunshine, talking, debating, laughing, without a care in the world. "These are the good times for them," he said, "the happy times. They're like guests at a wedding, keeping the bridegroom company - celebrating. Time enough for fasting and being sad after the bridegroom has gone. As for your cherished religious traditions . . . they were right in the old days. But I've come to teach new ways. New ideas can't be squeezed to fit in with old laws. You don't patch old clothes with new cloth, do you? Or put new wine into old wineskins - the skins split! No. New bottles for new wine, I say. A new way of living for a new sort of life."

When Jesus heard it, he saith unto them, They that are whole have no need of the physician, but they that are sick: I came not to call the righteous, but sinners to repentance.

MARK 2:17

BREAKING THE SABBATH

IT WAS A VERY STRICT AND ANCIENT LAW among the Jews that the Sabbath - that last day of the week, when God rested from making the world - should be entirely given over to worship. Men should do no work in the fields, women no cooking or cleaning at home.

Now the Pharisees were so determined to find fault with Jesus and his disciples that they followed him about, watching for the least little mistake to pounce on, like jackals stalking antelope, watching for a weakness in the herd. One Sabbath, the disciples, walking through a ripe field of corn, casually picked some ears of corn, rubbed them between their palms, then nibbled the loose grains.

"Aha!" crowed the Pharisees. "How is it you let your disciples break the Sabbath by *milling corn* between their hands? Eh? Eh?"

Jesus gently reminded them of King David who, once upon a time, had gone into a synagogue and eaten the consecrated bread off the holy altar and given it to his men to eat, because they were all hungry and in need of it. And who were they to criticize the great King David? "The Sabbath was made for *our* benefit, not the other way round!"

That same day Jesus went to preach in the synagogue. There was a man there whose arm was shrivelled up and useless. Obviously he was hoping Jesus would cure him as he had cured so many others. But there lurked the Pharisees, rubbing their hands with glee and thinking, "Will he break the Sabbath to cure this man? Then we'll have him! Working on the Sabbath!"

Jesus guessed what they were thinking and, appalled they should care so little about the man himself, looked them in the eye and asked, "Which does your holy Law say I should do on the Sabbath:

And he said unto them, The Sabbath was made for man, and not man for the Sabbath . . .

MARK 2:27

good or bad? Does it say I should save life or take life away?" No answer. "If a sheep of yours fell in a ditch on the Sabbath, is there a single one of you who would stand by and let the poor beast die rather than pull it out - *because of the Law?* And isn't a man more valuable than a sheep?"

Still they did not answer, those calculating, uncharitable men. So Jesus told the man with the thin, dangling, useless arm, "Stretch out your hand."

The hand that reached out to take Jesus's was as plump and strong and perfect as its partner: the man was healed.

And what did the Pharisees do? They immediately began to mutter and scheme among themselves, thinking of ways to spoil Christ's popularity with the people, plotting to destroy his work, even his life. That was how much he threatened their power and influence and comfortable way of life.

"We know just how he casts out demons!" they began telling people. "He's in league with the Devil himself!"

When Jesus heard this latest rumour he called the Pharisees to him and asked them, "How can the Devil overthrow himself? Why should he? Why *should* the Devil cast out demons? I ask you! It's not sensible. If the Devil is at work in me, and I use my power to destroy evil - well! there's an end to the Devil, wouldn't you say? Have a care, gentlemen. God can forgive every sin except one - and that's the sin of spreading lies about the Holy Spirit."

And the Pharisees went forth, and straightway took counsel with the Herodians against him, how they might destroy him.
MARK 3:6

CALMING THE STORM

ONE DAY, as on many days, Jesus and his disciples took a voyage over the Sea of Galilee. He had been teaching and travelling, travelling and teaching day in, day out, and he was very tired. No sooner had the boat slipped out into deep water than he curled up in the stern, on a pile of fishing nets, and fell fast asleep.

Now the Sea of Galilee may not be a true sea - only a big lake. But it is a very, very big lake. And behind the hills which surround it, lurk winds and squalls, like bandits lying in ambush. A storm can sweep down without a moment's warning, and whip the lake into a maelstrom.

Suddenly, the sky above Jesus's boat turned a sickly yellow and the temperature dropped. A squall of wind pounced on the lake and gouged the smooth water into huge, white-topped waves. Before the men could lower the sail, it was torn to rags at the masthead. The little boat began to pitch and roll. Green glassy mountains of water heaved themselves high above the bulwarks and smashed down on the disciples, making them stagger and choke, filling the bilges with swilling cold water. Spray dashed itself in their faces. They were terrified.

Even the fishermen among them were afraid, for they knew how many little boats had been swallowed up by such storms. The boards groaned, the swell threw the boat in the air only to drop it into the next deep trough with a hollow thud. It rode lower and lower in the water.

And all this while, Jesus slept, as peacefully as baby Moses rocked in his basket of reeds.

"Wake up, Master! Wake up! We're sinking!" gasped the disciples. "We're going down! We'll have to swim for it!"

And there arose a great storm of wind, and the waves beat into the ship, so that it was now full. And he was in the hinder part of the ship, asleep on a pillow: and they awake him, and say unto him, Master, carest thou not that we perish?

MARK 4:37, 38

by sentence, to those at the back who were murmuring, "What did he say? I missed that. Tell us what he said."

Later, those people maybe met up with friends or relations in the next town, exchanged news, jokes, stories - including the tales they had heard from Jesus - the one about the overseer, the one about the rich man, the one about the woman who lost a coin from her headband. They were easy to remember, and so easy to pass on.

The Gospel writers probably only recorded their favourites. There must have been more. A good story weathers the passage of time, and the stories Jesus told have survived for thousands of years. Because the messages within them - about the way people are, the things they do, and the way they tackle life's day-to-day problems - are just as true now as on the day the stories were first told.

THE SOWER

One day, the crowds which gathered round Jesus were so huge that he was being jostled and squeezed too much even to speak. So he got into a boat and sat in the prow, his feet dangling, the reflected sunlight playing on his face from below. The crowd spread out round the lakeside. Some sat down painfully on thistles. Some crushed the corn on the edge of a farmer's field. Jesus began to tell this story:

A farmer went out to sow wheat, tossing the grain ahead of him and to either side, in a cascade of golden seed. Some of the grains missed the field altogether and landed on the path where the birds pecked them up. Some fell on stony ground and shallow soil, put down eager roots and sprouted, but then wilted and drooped in the hot sun for lack of moisture. Some fell among weeds, and the weeds choked the young shoots. But some took root in rich, fertile soil, and grew up strong and tall. At harvest time, these stalks were bent heavy under ears of twenty seeds, fifty seeds, a hundred.

And some fell among thorns, and the thorns grew up, and choked it, and it yielded no fruit.

MARK 4:7

The word of God is like that. Sometimes it does not even get a hearing. Sometimes it fires a wild enthusiasm . . . which somehow fades when the initial excitement wears off. Sometimes good intentions are choked by other concerns - money, family, work . . . And there again, sometimes it sinks in, is given the chance to grow, and may spread God's influence to twenty, fifty or a hundred other lives.

A WASTER OF A SON

There were always families among the listening crowds. Sometimes a little child might wander off and get lost and have to be found. A toddler sitting in the shade of a tree might stuff one of the seed pods into its mouth and be smacked. "Ugh! Nasty. Only fit for pigs! Spit it out." Sometimes sisters would start arguing - or a mother would suddenly look sad because her children, grown up and gone from home, would not hear this marvellous teacher . . . Everyone has a family. Everyone knows what ups and downs families go through . . .

A rich man had two sons - John and Jack. John was a good, dutiful boy, but Jack was wilder, and took it into his head to leave home. So he asked his father for his share of the family money: "Whatever I'm due to inherit, since I won't be around here when you die."

The father, for all he did not want his son to go, gave him what he asked.

With the money in his pocket, Jack felt free to travel and live life to the full. He gambled, flaunted his money in front of women to impress them, dressed in expensive clothes and frequently drank himself into a stupor. One day, he put his hand in his pocket to buy bread . . . and there was no money. What is more, there was no bread. The country where he found himself was racked with famine. Before the famine was done, Jack was forced to take work as a pigman, feeding swill to the animals. He even envied the pigs their disgusting slops.

"What am I doing here?" he said to a sow, one day. "My father's servants don't starve, or sleep in a handful of dirty hay like I do. I'll go home. I've forfeited any right to call myself his son, but Father might be willing to give me a job if I go down on my knees . . ."

Jack did not need to go down on his knees. While he was still

I will arise and go to my father, and will say unto him, Father, I have sinned against heaven, and before thee, and am no more worthy to be called thy son: make me as one of thy hired servants.

Luke 15:18-19

a long way off, his father recognized his shabby, stooping figure limping homeward, and ran to meet him and hugged him and kissed him and wept salt tears of happiness over his dirty face. Jack began his prepared speech: "I'm know I'm not worthy to be your son, but if I could just work . . ." But his father would have none of it. "Bring a new suit of clothes and prepare a feast!" he told the servants. "My son has come home!"

Jack's brother John was less delighted. "Here I am - obedient, hard-working, never putting a foot wrong. And when do I get a feast thrown for me, eh?"

His father gave him a reproving, sidelong look. "Any time, any day, son. You only have to ask. Try not to be bitter. I thought I'd never see Jack again - and here he is, home again and glad to be home. Isn't that reason enough to be happy?"

Jesus said, more than once, that he had come for the sake of sinners, not good, sober, respectable, religious folk. Sometimes that can seem a bit hard on good, sober, respectable folk doing their best to lead decent lives. But look at it this way. A person given over to wildness and wrong is temporarily lost to God, out of earshot of His voice. And since God loves us all like a father, is it surprising if He longs to see His lost children stumbling home, older and wiser? And no one's perfect. We can all afford to be glad that God is able to forgive just about anything once He is asked.

And bring hither the fatted calf, and kill it; and let us eat, and be merry: For this my son was dead, and is alive again; he was lost, and is found. And they began to be merry.

LUKE 15:23, 24

THE GOOD SHEPHERD

Above the murmur of the crowd and the lapping of the lake on the shore, there was often the sound of sheep and goats bleating on nearby hillsides, while Jesus talked. The shepherds tended to keep well away from the crowds - silent, solitary men by dint of long days and nights spent alone minding livestock; thoughtful

*I am the good
shepherd, and
know my sheep,
and am known of
mine. As the
Father knoweth
me, even so know
I the Father: and
I lay down my life
for the sheep.*
JOHN 10:14, 15

men, none the less, with plenty of time to think. Everyone knew that a good, watchful shepherd was a great asset to a landowner.

A shepherd had one hundred sheep in the morning, when he set them free to graze, but only ninety-six, ninety-seven, ninety-eight, ninety-nine in the evening, when he gathered them into the safety of the fold. The sun had set, there were wolves howling in the darkness, and a keen frost was creeping over the hills. The shepherd's fire was already lit, he was hungry and tired. But nevertheless, he fastened the gate of the fold securely and, taking his crook, walked off through the twilight, searching. He did not *need* to. One sheep is no great loss, to a man with ninety-nine others. Most shepherds would not have bothered about just one. And it was dangerous out there, after dark, with the wolves running.

But then, reasoned the good shepherd, so was it dangerous for the lost sheep. Would the darkness be smothering her even now with fear and freezing dew? So the shepherd went searching, and he did not stop till he heard a forlorn bleat coming from a high ledge, and found his lost sheep, snagged in a thornbush.

It is the same with God, Jesus was saying. No one is expendable. No one can be abandoned to their fate, unloved, just because they have wandered a long way off course and fallen into a whole toil of trouble. In fact Jesus called himself "The Good Shepherd", because it was he whom God sent into the cold, dangerous, dingy world to find and rescue the weak, the ones who have been given up for lost.

THE LOST COIN

It was the same for the woman whose headband of coins broke. A frayed thread, a snap, and the ten silver coins her husband had given her on their wedding day went scattering and rolling across the floor. In contrast with the bright daylight outside, the house was pitch dark. The floor was strewn with straw. But by lighting a lamp and feeling about, the woman managed to find nine of the coins.

If she threaded them on to a new thread, her husband would never notice one was gone; nine is nearly as good as ten. But the woman just *knew* that tenth coin was somewhere, and she refused to stop looking. She got out a broom and swept the whole house - and suddenly, there under the broomhead, was a glint of silver.

Well, she danced on the spot and she danced on the steps and she danced on the roof of her clean little house. When her neighbours went by, she called down to them, "I found it! I did! I found that coin I lost!" so that the neighbours smiled to think anyone should go to so much trouble over one little coin.

But it was no more than the trouble God goes to, after all, to fetch back people who had strayed away from Him. And Heaven celebrates just as much when the lost are found.

WHO DO I HAVE TO LIKE?

When Jesus told his disciples to forgive their fellow creatures, the disciples wanted to know how many times, how many crimes they had to forgive. Three? Five? Seven?

"Seventy times seven," said Jesus.

When Jesus told his disciples to love their neighbours, the disciples wanted to know who qualified as a neighbour. Close family? The people in the same street? The same town? Or tribe?

Jesus answered with this story:

A man was travelling down to Jericho, the comfortable sway and jolt of his donkey lulling him to sleep. The sun was low in his eyes. Suddenly, a rock hit him squarely on the forehead and he

. . . what woman having ten pieces of silver, if she lose one piece, doth not light a candle, and sweep the house, and seek diligently till she find it?
LUKE 15:8

. . . Rejoice with me; for I have found the piece which I had lost.
LUKE 15:9

STORIES JESUS TOLD

And Jesus answering said, A certain man went down from Jerusalem to Jericho, and fell among thieves, which stripped him of his raiment, and wounded him, and departed, leaving him half dead.

LUKE 10:30

reeled in the saddle. Hands grabbed the back of his robe, pulling him down. Fists were pummelling him, feet kicking him. A knife flashed in the sun. He put up a struggle, but there were half a dozen of them - bandits preying on travellers along that lonely, isolated road. They dragged his donkey away braying, its legs stiff, its hoofs catching the man on the ground. And when they had checked the saddlebags, they came back and searched him for any money in his pockets, any clothes they might sell at a profit. More dead than alive, he lay, flyblown, in the hot sun, praying for someone to come along before heat and thirst finished what the bandits had begun.

A priest came by. But robbery is an unpleasant business. People getting injured is *so* upsetting, and the priest did not like to think of nasty, unhappy things. So when he saw the traveller, the blood, the gathering flies, he crossed the road to the other side, and hurried by.

A good Jewish boy, the pride of his mother, came by and saw the injured man. He would have liked to stop and help. But supposing the bandits were still about? Supposing they jumped out from behind that rock and did the same thing to him? What good would he be then, to his mother and friends? Better to hurry on by, on the other side of the road.

The injured man, seeing help pass him by, turned his face to the sky and despaired. His strength was fading; come nightfall, the cruel heat of the day would give way to the crueller cold. He would never see the morning.

Just then a Samaritan came down the same stretch of road.

(At this point in the story, some of those listening spat on the ground: in Judaea, the people of Samaria were held in about as much esteem as earwigs or large rats.)

This Samaritan saw the kites circling in the sky, saw the bundle of clothes huddled below the rocks, saw the blood. He ran to the injured man and gave him water from a skin bag. "Quiet now. I'll take care of you. No need to worry." With a glance in the direction of the rocks, terrified of the bandits returning, he nevertheless took off his undershirt and tore it into strips for bandages, then gently lifted the man on to his donkey and led the animal, at the very gentlest pace, to an inn further down the road.

As he entered, several customers naturally got up and moved away, so as not to brush shoulders with a Samaritan.

"Innkeeper, I found this man on the road. Will you look after him for me until I've finished my business and I can get back here? Look, here's money to pay for anything you need - food, medicine. I'll give you more when I come back, if he has put you to any extra expense." And the innkeeper took the money (though he polished it on his apron afterwards, to remove any taint of Samaritan).

It cost the Samaritan a tidy sum - cost him time and effort, too, and made him late home. But he had done what he felt he must, to help a fellow creature.

At the end of the story, Jesus looked about him at the listening faces and asked, "Who do *you* think was a true neighbour to the injured man?" The listeners were slow to answer, but not because they did not know. "Everyone is your neighbour," said Jesus. "Loving just the ones you like isn't enough. Anyone can do that."

Which now of these three, thinkest thou, was neighbour unto him that fell among the thieves? And he said, He that shewed mercy on him. Then said Jesus unto him, Go, and do thou likewise.

LUKE 10:36, 37

THE HOUSE-BUILDERS

What a number of houses Jesus must have slept in as he wandered the countryside, or stopped for a midday meal: one night a big, two-storey villa with balconies and outside stairs, grapes drying

Therefore whosoever heareth these sayings of mine, and doeth them, I will liken him unto a wise man, which built his house upon a rock: And the rain descended, and the floods came, and the winds blew, and beat upon that house; and it fell not: for it was founded upon a rock.

MATTHEW 7:24, 25

Then said he, Unto what is the Kingdom of God like? and whereunto shall I resemble it?

LUKE 13:18

on the flat roof; one day a simple, one-room place, pitch dark but blessedly cool for want of windows, a loom in one corner, a table in the other, straw on the floor, and an oil lamp burning . . .

Two men set out to build houses. One built his on rock, with a firm foundation, so that when the wind blew and the rain rained, the house stood up to it all, and gave him shelter from the storm.

The other man built his house on the beach: he had always wanted to live near the sea. It was a good house - nothing slapdash - he took great care in the building of it. But when the rain rained, and puddles grew into streams, and streams into floods, when rivers burst their banks and the sea rose on a wild spring tide, the sand beneath the house shifted, crawled away, let him down. The house fell down with a noise like a shipwreck.

A person's life is built like a house. If it doesn't have firm foundations, where are you going to shelter when the wind blows and the rain rains, and times grow dangerous and raw?

OUT OF SMALL BEGINNINGS

"But what is the Kingdom of God like?" they asked Jesus all the time. "What is it like?" Perhaps they expected descriptions of palaces sublime beyond imagination, floating in the clouds. Perhaps they expected monumental mansions teetering on remote mountain tops. But Jesus likened the Kingdom to things far less grand and far more marvellous.

"The Kingdom of God is like a mustard seed," he said.

A mustard seed? Tinier than a freckle, or a fleck of grit?

"A man once took a single mustard seed and planted it in his garden," said Jesus. "It sprouted. It grew. It flourished. When it was fully grown . . ." and he looked beyond them to where a mustard tree spread like the veins in an eye, but so immense that it half filled the sky, ". . . all the birds of every kind found room to perch in its branches."

The crowd gasped, as if they had just glimpsed the spires of Heaven.

"The Kingdom of God is like the leaven in a loaf of bread," said Jesus.

Leaven? Yeast? That grey, mouldy, smelly, two-palmfuls-a-penny ingredient every housewife kept by her stove?

"A woman took one tiny pinch one day, and divided it in three. It was still enough. And before the oven was hot . . ." Jesus broke open a large, plump loaf of bread, and the crowd savoured its delicious, fresh-baked smell ". . . before the oven was hot, three lumps of dough had swelled into loaves big enough to feed her whole family."

The crowd nodded. They knew it was true. Listening to Jesus they could feel understanding swell inside them like yeast, and happiness settle on to them like birds out of a singing sky.

It is like a grain of mustard seed, which a man took, and cast into his garden; and it grew, and waxed a great tree; and the fowls of the air lodged in the branches of it.

LUKE 13:19

PARTY INVITATIONS

One night Jesus and his disciples sat down to dinner with a rich Pharisee. It was a good dinner, they were glad of it; glad, too, of a story from Jesus. He waved a hand in the direction of the delicious food and said that it put him in mind of the wedding feast where nobody came.

A king sent out invitations to all the important people in his kingdom: *Come to a feast to celebrate my son's marriage!*

Oddly enough, they all seemed to have something better to do. One sent word that he had bought a new team of oxen and wanted to put them to work ploughing a field.

One had bought a new piece of land a long way away, and was travelling there to look it over.

Then saith he to his servants, The wedding is ready, but they which were bidden were not worthy.

MATTHEW 22:8

One explained that he had just got married. Perhaps it was his wife who said she could not spare him. But you would have thought they would both have remembered their own wedding feast and the joy of having their friends around them, wishing them well.

When this catalogue of miserable excuses reached the ears of the king, he was deeply insulted. "In that case, go out into the market-places and alleyways, and invite all the poorest, loneliest, most unfortunate people you can lay your hands on!" he told his servants. "*They'll* be glad enough to come!"

And so they were. The blind, the crippled, the beggars off the street corners, the orphans and the homeless could hardly believe their luck. They showered the king with thanks as they showered the bridegroom with flower petals. For months afterwards it was all they could talk about - the food, the music, the dancing, the honour! "What did we do to deserve it?" they never tired of asking. "That was a feast to remember!"

For many are called, but few are chosen.

MATTHEW 22:14

The disciples must have been very glad then that they had followed Jesus so wholeheartedly. God's invitation is open to everyone, but it has to be accepted in the right spirit - taken for what it is: the single most important thing in life, coming before everything and everyone else. Otherwise the door will close, and the place at God's table go to someone more deserving.

VIEWS FROM A MOUNTAINSIDE

ONE MEMORABLE DAY, Jesus spoke to the crowds from a mountainside, sitting amid the skirts of his robes, surrounded by disciples. They plucked lazily at the grass, while moths staggered through sunlight laden with the scent of wild flowers. He told them who the world's truly lucky people were - the ones who would fare best. Around him was written on each listening face, "Am I like that? Am I that kind of person?" The lucky ones he described were not what you would expect: those desperate for spiritual understanding, the sad, the meek, the honest and straightforward, the peacemakers, those who suffer for the sake of what they believe. "It may be hard for them in this life," said Jesus, 'but just wait till they see what rewards God has in store for them! You who understand what I'm saying - you're the salt that gives life its flavour! You're the light that lights up the world for other people. Don't make a secret of it! Shine!"

Then, amazingly, Jesus took the old Judaic Law set down by the great men of old, and turned it on its head. "If someone injures you, he must be made to suffer for it, that's what the law says, isn't it? Well, I say, if someone slaps you on one cheek, offer him the other to slap too! If a Roman soldier pressgangs you into carrying his luggage one mile . . ." (The crowd groaned and nodded; they had all had to do that.) ". . . I say, go another mile out of the goodness of your heart! It's not enough just to love your own family and friends - everyone does that. Now you have to love and forgive everyone, without reservation, as God does. Even your worst enemy.

"But don't make a big show of being 'religious' - not like those hypocrites you see in the Temple sometimes: 'Look at me! Look at how good I am! Thank goodness I'm so much better

---

Blessed are the poor in spirit: for theirs is the kingdom of heaven. Blessed are they that mourn: for they shall be comforted. Blessed are the meek: for they shall inherit the earth. Blessed are they which do hunger and thirst after righteousness: for they shall be filled. Blessed are the merciful: for they shall obtain mercy. Blessed are the pure in heart: for they shall see God. Blessed are the peacemakers: for they shall be called the children of God.

MATTHEW 5:3-12

than that miserable fellow over there!' " The listening crowds rolled with laughter in the grass. They knew the sort: giving out charity like royalty, shouting prayers into the rafters to outdo the man alongside.

"Well then, teach us how to pray," said his disciples.

So Jesus taught them the outlines of a prayer they could use every day, one which would bring God closer while they said it:

"Our Father in Heaven, may your name always be held in reverence. May you soon rule Earth as you do Heaven, and may we carry out your wishes as willingly as the angels do now. Please give us what we need to keep body and soul together today, and forgive us what we do wrong. If possible, don't let us even be tempted to do wrong, and please spare us coming face-to-face with wickedness."

"Whatever you prize most," said Jesus, "you will spend most time and effort on. If it's worldly things, like money, fame, security, then that's what you'll chase after. God will get pushed into second place. So don't worry about where the next meal is coming from, or how you are going to afford a new coat. Don't you think God can take care of all that? Look around you!" Exquisite poppies danced in robes of scarlet velvet, as splendid as any king. Birds sang on the spiny branches with not a care in the world. "Let tomorrow take care of itself," said Jesus. "Take one day at a time." They believed him. After all, he was not asking anything of them that he was not prepared to do himself.

After this manner therefore pray ye: Our Father which art in heaven, Hallowed be thy name. Thy kingdom come. Thy will be done in earth, as it is in heaven. Give us this day our daily bread. And forgive us our debts, as we forgive our debtors. And lead us not into temptation, but deliver us from evil: For thine is the kingdom, and the power, and the glory, for ever. Amen.

MATTHEW 6:9-13

THE LITTLE GIRL WHO DIED

JAIRUS WAS A MAN of great importance, presiding over a synagogue. But he must have been rather a different man from his fellow Pharisees and scribes, must have seen more to Jesus than a threat. Or perhaps a man's love for his child overcomes all his prejudices, just as Jesus's love for people forgave all their faults. When Jairus's twelve-year-old daughter fell ill, he would have beat on the very gates of Heaven to keep her from dying. As his wife sobbed and tore her clothes, as the neighbours gathered in dismal clusters round the door, all Jairus could think of was Jesus the Healer - the man who worked miracles. Pausing only to kiss his daughter's clammy forehead, he lunged for the door, scattering the neighbours and pelting through the streets in search of the man from Nazareth.

Rounding the corner, he found his way barred by throngs of people, some of whom fell back respectfully at the sight of him. "Come quick! Please!" he begged Jesus. "My little girl . . ." and he began to tug Jesus along, imploring him to hurry.

But before they reached Jairus's house, another member of his family came to find them, his headdress crammed against his mouth, his face wet with tears. "I'm sorry, Jairus. It's too late. Leave the Master in peace. Your daughter is already . . ."

"*NO!*" Jairus stood stock still. His face turned grey. His legs shook. When Jesus laid a hand on his shoulder, he mistook it for sympathy, fatuous, futile sympathy. It was not. "Take no notice," Jesus said in Jairus's ear. "Just have faith."

The house was full of women wailing and tossing their hair like horses' manes, in paroxysms of grief. Jesus shooed them out of doors. "Why all the tears?" he asked. "The girl's just asleep." They stared back at him out of unseeing, red-rimmed eyes.

. . . My daughter is even now dead: but come and lay thy hand upon her, and she shall live.
MATTHEW 9:18

. . . Give place: for the maid is not dead, but sleepeth.
MATTHEW 9:24

Only Jairus and his wife were allowed to follow Jesus into the room where the little girl lay, eyes shut, white as death. Jesus picked up one limp, cold hand. "Get up, little lamb," he whispered. She opened her eyes and smiled at him.

The parents, dumbfounded, watched their daughter sit up and set her feet to the floor, as though she had slept deep and was still in the grip of a dream. Fraily at first, and then more steadily, she walked around the room, leaning on Jesus's arm. He whispered something to her which made her laugh out loud - a sound which set Jairus's heart clamouring like a gong. Then Jesus saw how they stood and stared, rooted to the spot. "Oh, do get her something to eat, won't you?" he exclaimed cheerfully. "Can't you see she's hungry?"

"Yes. Of course. Straight away. Oh! Oh, Jairus! Food. Yes. Exactly. Oh!" said the mother, plucking shyly at the rents in her clothes as she hurried out to the oven. But Jairus stood with his back to the bedroom wall, while the world rolled under his feet. If his daughter was alive again, then he was more than alive, he was born anew into a world full of colour and happiness and the most amazing possibilities.

WICKED WOMEN

THERE WERE WOMEN, too, among Jesus's friends. Although they were not free to wander the countryside in quite the same way, they hung just as fervently on his words. Their shrewd eyes saw deep into his character, and found it perfect. One woman had especially good reason to love him: he saved her life.

Jesus was teaching in the Temple one day when the scribes and Pharisees dragged before him - like some sacrificial sheep - a woman all tousled and tear-stained. "This worthless creature is a sinner," they brayed disdainfully. "She has broken our law and must be stoned to death. Mustn't she?"

What did they want him to say? "Stone her", so they could throw in his face his talk of mercy and forgiveness? "Forgive her"? Then they could say that he did not believe in people obeying the law. Jesus looked at the woman crouching crumpled on the ground; she looked back at him, imploring.

At first, he did not seem interested in answering - just drew with his finger on the dusty floor. Then he said, "Let the man who has never sinned himself throw the first stone." And he went on making loops and circles in the dust with his finger.

When he looked up next, no one remained but the woman herself. Every one of her accusers had recalled some sin so black on his conscience that he squirmed with guilt, and crept silently away. "What, no one left to condemn you?" The woman shook her head. "Then I don't condemn you either."

Young Salome, by contrast, was adored by everyone. She was stepdaughter and niece to King Herod Antipas, daughter of his queen.

Now Queen Herodias, before marrying the King, had been married to his brother, and that, according to Jewish law, was all

. . . He that is without sin among you, let him first cast a stone at her.
JOHN 8:7

wrong. Part of the reason why John the Baptist had been put in prison was that he had told Herod, in no uncertain terms, that he ought not to have married Herodias. Herod took no notice, of course, although he faintly admired John's courage. But Herodias detested the "wilderness" preacher for daring to criticize her. When Herodias could not persuade Herod to execute John, she resorted to slyer means.

One night, during a splendid feast, young Salome danced for Herod. She was a marvellous dancer, lithe and passionate. She whirled and arched her back, bare feet slapping the marble floor, the fine tissue of her clothing enveloping her like flame. Herod leaned forward on his throne, entranced. When Salome finished, he vowed she should have anything - any reward she cared to ask for. "Name it!" he chortled. "Name it!"

Straight away Herodias whispered in her daughter's ear. Salome swallowed hard, and turned a little pale. But she did as her mother told her. "Let my reward be the head of John the Baptist on a

And she, being before instructed of her mother, said, Give me here John Baptist's head in a charger.

MATTHEW 14:8

silver platter!" she said. Herod's face fell. Everyone in the room was looking at him. He could not retract his kingly promise. There was a sickening lull in the evening's festivities, while a message was sent to the prison, and everyone waited, and nobody spoke. Then a servant brought in a silver platter - just as he might another course of the meal . . . except that this platter bore a man's head. The servant carried it to Salome, who gave it hastily to her mother. Herod looked at the smile on his wife's face, her hands gripping that grotesque plate in her lap . . . Perhaps, after this, he would not be able to look at her in quite the same light ever again.

"Who do people say that I am?" asked Jesus of his disciple Simon Peter.

"Some say you are the prophet Elijah come again. Or Elisha. Some say you are John the Baptist brought back to life."

Jesus looked away, towards the Jordan, where John his cousin had held him in his arms in the act of baptizing him.

"And who do *you* say that I am?" asked Jesus.

"I say you are the Christ. The Messiah. The Saviour."

It was what John the Baptist had said as well. But now John would not live to see it proved to the world.

A MEAL FOR FIVE THOUSAND

ON ONE OF THOSE CROWDED, milling days, the hours slipped away unnoticed, and found Jesus, his disciples and a townful of people still together at sunset. "Shouldn't we send them into town to buy supper for themselves?" asked the disciples.

"Why? Can't we offer them something to eat?" asked Jesus, for all the world as if a few unexpected guests had called, and supper would have to stretch a little further.

"But we only have . . ." They rummaged in their deep, flapping pockets. Empty. They turned towards the people nearest in the crowd. "Do you have any . . . ?" And the crowd, shrugging, holding up empty hands, turned to the people behind them. A murmur ran over an acre of faces. Then a little boy on tiptoe, shy and embarrassed, called out, "I have five loaves and this couple of fish!" The paltry provisions were handed forward, the fish looking even sorrier by the time they arrived in Jesus's hands.

He took the loaves and fish in the skirt of his robe, as if showing them to the sky. "Bless, Lord, this meal of ours," he said, and

*And he commanded
the multitude to sit
down on the grass,
and took the five
loaves, and the two
fishes, and looking
up to heaven, he
blessed, and brake,
and gave the loaves
to his disciples, and
the disciples to the
multitude. And
they did all eat . . .
And they that had
eaten were about
five thousand men,
beside women
and children.*
MATTHEW 14:19,
20, 21

the disciples mumbled something similar. "Now everyone – sit down!"

He broke the food into chunks, and sent the disciples in among the crowds, who settled themselves in circles on the grass: family groups, bands of friends, those who had met during the long, happy day. Perhaps they too had scraps in their pockets to share with each other. Perhaps some of the five thousand also contributed to the gigantic picnic. But everyone dipped into that basket of loaves and fishes, and everyone ate.

So how come, when the scraps were gathered up afterwards by the disciples (who hated to see good food go to waste), there were twelve baskets of crumbs and fish-heads, bones and crumbled crust? Because a miracle had happened? Because everyone shared what they had? Because God smiled on their sharing?

WALKING ON WATER

BEFORE THE GREAT PICNIC had finally disbanded, Jesus told the disciples to set sail across the Sea of Galilee, while he said goodbye to the last of the five thousand. "How will you catch us up?" they asked, but Jesus had already turned away.

When he was finally alone, Jesus walked to a hilltop and prayed. And when he had finished praying, he walked down again - down the grassy slope, now deserted, the grass flattened by five thousand feet, across the rocky beach, on to where the water broke against the shore in white surf. And then on further still.

Meanwhile, a keen wind had sprung up, and the disciples, though a good half-mile from shore, were making little headway. The swell was heavy, the waves menacing. At first, they thought they were seeing spray scuffed up off the crests of the waves. But then they saw it had the shape of a man, and were panicstricken. "A ghost! A ghost! If only Jesus were here! He never told us how to cope with ghosts!" They wanted to look, they did not dare to. The spectral man trod boldly from wave to wave.

"Don't fret!" he called. "It's only me."

The boat hove to, while the disciples rushed up and down, grabbing each other by the sleeve and gasping, "Walking on the water! Do you see? He is, isn't he? He's walking on water!"

Suddenly it struck some of them that this might not be Jesus at all, but a demon in disguise (the Devil is always out to trick people).

"If it is you, Lord, tell me to come to you over the water," said Peter. He was excited, eyes bright, cheeks flushed. "Tell me to come." Jesus beckoned him.

Bundling his robes up in one hand, Peter scrambled over the rail, eager to see what it felt like - to walk on water! The sea took

. . . Jesus went unto them, walking on the sea. And when the disciples saw him walking on the sea, they were troubled, saying, It is a spirit; and they cried out for fear.
MATTHEW 14:25, 26

his weight. He set each foot on the black waves and felt them, like a springy garden bed of newly turned earth, under his sandals.

"But it's water," he thought. "Rough water, too. And men can't walk on . . ." As his faith failed, he began to sink. Jesus was reaching out encouraging hands, but Peter began to sink, because what he was doing was impossible. In that moment, he thought he was about to drown. "Lord, save me!"

"Oh, how little faith you have!" Jesus reproached Peter. "Why did you start to *doubt* me?"

Together, they climbed into the boat. The wind dropped. The sea fell flat, flat as spilled oil. Then Peter began to regret his lack of faith. What might he have done with more faith? But no, he had doubted. He had taken fright. Worst of all, he had failed Jesus, and rather than do that, he would have walked across half the oceans of the world.

Around Jesus, the other disciples fell to their knees. "No doubt about it," they said. "No question. You're the Son of God."

WALKING ON
WATER

But when he saw the wind boisterous, he was afraid; and beginning to sink, he cried, saying, Lord, save me. And immediately Jesus stretched forth his hand, and caught him, and said unto him, O thou of little faith, wherefore didst thou doubt?
MATTHEW 14: 30, 31

VISITORS FROM THE PAST

THE DISCIPLES SAW so many wonders: the blind able to see, the insane cured, even a man walking on water. But nothing prepared them for the sight they saw one day on a mountain top. Peter, James and John had gone with Jesus - high up where the only tracks were made by sheep and lambs. Jesus was walking on ahead.

Suddenly a change overtook him. Despite the dust and grime of travel, and all the hands which had grabbed pleadingly at him, Jesus's clothes began to shine - whiter than any cloth or cloud or snowstorm. The sunlight became entangled in the very weave of his robe and strands of his hair, so that Jesus himself shone. Once he had called himself "The Light of the World": all of a sudden, he was. His face was dazzling bright - and he was not alone.

Two figures walked alongside him, and all three were deep in conversation. Peter, James and John knew instantly who the new-comers were. How? How could they recognize men long since dead - men from the dawning of history? They simply *knew* that it was Elijah the prophet and Moses, father of the Jewish nation.

Peter gave a groan. This was stupendous, momentous, earth-shattering! It was a moment which cracked Time and shook the history of the world . . . And he could not think what to do about it. Should he build an altar? Should he pile up rocks to mark the place? Should he raise shelters to shield those noble heads from the beating sun? "Shall I? Should I? What must I do?"

But it was not Peter's place to do anything: simply to see, to remember, and to hear. A limb of cloud swung over the mountain like an arm extended in blessing. And a voice echoed among the rocks: *"This is my son: he has pleased me greatly."*

Then Peter stood still and stared. The spirits of the past melted

And he was transfigured before them: and his face did shine as the sun, and his raiment was white as the light.
MATTHEW 17:2

While he yet spake, behold, a bright cloud overshadowed them: and behold a voice out of the cloud, which said, This is my beloved Son, in whom I am well pleased; hear ye him.
MATTHEW 17:5

away: Elijah and Moses were gone. No one was left but Jesus, walking back towards his friends. "Don't say anything about what you saw here today," said Jesus. "Not yet, anyway."

Dumbly the disciples nodded. Of course they would not tell anyone. It was not plain in their own minds what they had seen, or why they had been permitted to see it. How could they tell others? It would sound far too much like boasting.

LITTLE MAN

ZACCHAEUS WAS A VERY *LITTLE* MAN. He did little for his neighbours except collect taxes from them for the Romans. He had a great deal of money, but little to be proud of in earning it. And he was liked very, very little by the people of Jericho where he lived. He was also four feet tall in his sandals, and as thin as a pin.

When Jesus came to town, Zacchaeus was intrigued to see the famous man for himself. But the crowds got in the way. Though he pushed and peeped and jumped up high, Zacchaeus could not so much as see the colour of Jesus's hair. No one made way for him: not for a tax-collector.

So Zacchaeus ran on ahead of the crowd, and climbed up a sycamore tree - quite a feat for the Chief Tax-Collector of Jericho, who was no youngster. Hidden amid the tree's leafy canopy, he ran little risk of being seen, but did have a first-rate view. "Here he comes. So that's what the famous Jesus looks like, is it?" Closer and closer came Jesus, swept along like a leaf on a river.

Under the sycamore tree, he stopped. "Zacchaeus! Hurry down from there, will you? I'm having supper with you tonight!"

And when Jesus came to the place, he looked up, and saw him, and said unto him, Zacchaeus, make haste, and come down; for today I must abide at thy house.
LUKE 19:5

The crowds looked around and behind them, puzzled. The only Zacchaeus they knew was the Chief Tax-Collector, and he was nowhere about. Jesus looked up into the tree. So did the crowd. There sat Zacchaeus, grinning sheepishly down, showing a yard of leg as he felt for a foothold. The crowd began to hiss and boo. "Eat supper with a tax-collector? Surely not?" they muttered disapprovingly.

"It's the sinner, not the saint, who needs my help," said Jesus.

And away they went, Jesus and Zacchaeus arm in arm, the little man jumping high as they walked, to say in Jesus's ear, "Today I'm going to give away half of everything I own! And if I've ever cheated anyone - and I have - I'll make amends." He was a man transformed, because, for the first time in years, someone had befriended him. In fact he felt ten feet tall.

THE BRINGER OF LIFE

THE PRIESTS, who saw their influence slipping away wanted, more and more, to silence Jesus. They threatened to stone him; they tried to arrest him, but could no more take hold of him than the sunlight. Jesus escaped to the wild places, on the banks of the Jordan, where John the Baptist had lived and preached. Then a message came from Bethany, just two miles outside Jerusalem.

"*Our brother, your dear friend Lazarus, is very ill. Please come,*" wrote Martha and Mary.

"He's in no danger," said Jesus, folding the note. And for two days he did nothing. But the sisters' news must have preyed on his mind, for all of a sudden, he was off to Bethany.

"With the Temple Jews wanting to stone you to death?" gasped the disciples. "You can't possibly go!"

"I won't die one minute before God intends," said Jesus. "Besides, my friend Lazarus has fallen asleep; I must wake him." Off he went, and the disciples, fully expecting to be stoned or arrested, went too. "May as well die with him, I suppose," said Thomas the Twin.

By the time they reached Bethany, Lazarus had been sleeping the sleep of death for four days. Dead and buried. Martha came out to meet Jesus. "If you'd been here, my brother would never have died," she said, but without rancour, without reproach.

"Your brother will rise from the dead," said Jesus.

"At the end of the world, yes, I know. But that doesn't seem much comfort just now."

"I am Life itself. If anyone believes in me, their spirit can never die. Do you believe that, Martha?"

Jesus said unto her, I am the resurrection, and the life: he that believeth in me, though he were dead, yet shall he live: And whosoever liveth and believeth in me shall never die. Believest thou this?

JOHN 11:25, 26

Martha nodded. "I believe you're the Saviour of the World," she said, then went indoors to where her sister Mary sat surrounded by well-wishers and mourners. "The Teacher's here," she whispered to Mary. "He's asking for you."

When Jesus saw Mary's inconsolable grief, he was moved to tears himself. Together, they walked to the tomb - a cave sealed with a stone. "Take away the stone," said Jesus.

"But Teacher . . . it's been four days already!"

"Take it away." They rolled away the stone, and Jesus called, "Lazarus, come out!" A shiver ran through the crowd. What would they see? A ghost? A walking corpse?

Then out of the cave came Lazarus - an unnerving sight, certainly, bandaged from head to foot in grave-clothes, but Lazarus even so, restored to life and to his sisters' hugs and kisses.

And when he thus had spoken, he cried with a loud voice, Lazarus, come forth. And he that was dead came forth, bound hand and foot with graveclothes: and his face was bound about with a napkin. Jesus saith unto them, Loose him, and let him go.
JOHN 11:43, 44

*THE BRINGER
OF LIFE*

*Then said Jesus,
Let her alone:
against the day
of my burying hath
she kept this. For
the poor always
ye have with you;
but me ye have
not always.*
JOHN 12:7, 8

After that - the ultimate miracle - people either adored Jesus or were terrified of him. A man who could raise the dead?

"When the Romans hear this 'magic man' is stirring up the Jews, they'll come down on us with fire and sword. He'll be the death of us all," said the Pharisees.

"You know nothing," said Caiaphas, the High Priest, pondering the problem, fingers drumming. His eyes rested on a dead dove, its neck wrung, lying ready for the sacrificial flame. "Jesus-bar-Joseph may well bring down death on his own head - but is that *such* a bad thing? One man, killed by the Romans for his religion? It may even serve to pull the Jewish nation together. Under my rule. Isn't that worth the spilling of one heroic trouble-maker's blood? Hm?"

So, ironically, in raising a man to life, Jesus made the authorities all the more determined to put him to death.

Mary and Martha, on the other hand, adored him. When Jesus next visited their house, Martha rushed about preparing a magnificent meal, whereas Mary sat at his feet and drank in his words. (Each found her own way of worshipping the Saviour.) Suddenly Mary jumped up, fetched a flask of fabulously expensive perfume, and poured it over Jesus's feet, wiping them dry with her hair.

"What a waste!" protested Judas Iscariot sanctimoniously. "That perfume could have been sold, and the money given to the poor!"

"Leave her alone," said Jesus, in a voice moved by emotion. "If she did but know it, she's anointing me for burial in place of Lazarus . . . Besides, the poor will always be here to be helped. You only have me for a few more days."

INTO
JERUSALEM

AT LONG LAST, their travels brought Jesus and his disciples back to Jerusalem. Jesus was about to enter the Holy City, a celebrity now, famous from end to end of the country. Thousands hung on his every word. So, would he enter on a kingly camel or a prancing white charger, in a chariot, or carried shoulder-high by his followers?

"Go to that village over there," he told his disciples. "You'll find a donkey tethered there, which no one has ever ridden before. Bring it. If anyone interferes, say, 'The Lord needs it'."

They found the donkey colt, restless and skittish, nostrils flaring, eyes rolling, exactly as he had said they would.

"Hoi! What you doing? That's not your animal!" a man protested, as the disciples untied it.

"Our Lord needs it," they replied. He shrugged and turned away.

So Jesus entered Jerusalem sitting on a mount so small that the hem of his robes trailed on the ground and he could have dragged his sandals through the dirt. It was a humble enough means of travel - and yet the crowds saw the colt for what it was: the mount of a king in peacetime - not the horse of war, but the donkey of peace. And they welcomed Jesus like a hero, like a king, like a bringer of peace and life after too much death and suffering.

Here in Jerusalem, Jesus-the-Magnificent would surely achieve what God had sent him to do. Drive out the Romans? Start a revolution? Make his bid for power? The people did not know. They only knew that he had the wisdom of Solomon, the magic of Elijah, the greatness of Moses. So they took off their robes, ripped the branches off palm trees, and carpeted the road ahead of

And the multitudes that went before, and that followed, cried, saying, Hosanna to the son of David: Blessed is he that cometh in the name of the Lord; Hosanna in the highest.
MATTHEW 21:9

the shy little colt. They brandished the green palm fronds like flags, cheering home their hero: "Hosanna! God's Kingdom is beginning right here on Earth! Hurrah! Hosanna!"

The disciples revelled in that glorious day. It was right. It was fitting. This was the way their dear master should be greeted. Ridiculous to think it could be any other way! Thus they chose to forget what Jesus had clearly told them: that in entering Jerusalem, he was going to his death.

THE LAST SUPPER

PASSOVER WAS COMING – one of the most important festivals in the Jewish year, a celebration oddly tinged with blood. Passover commemorates that night in Eygpt when the Angel of Death passed over the Israelites and let them live, while all around, he slew the first-born sons of the Egyptians, and the sound of Egyptian mothers crying made the night quake. At Passover, Jewish families gather together, to eat and drink and celebrate being alive . . . though, of course, Death is a part of what they are celebrating.

To Jesus, the disciples were his true family, and it was with them that he spent Passover. They rented an upstairs room, somewhere to enjoy each other's company and a simple supper: a flat loaf of bread cooked without yeast (because that was how the Israelites baked it that night), a jug of wine, some fruit. A dish of salt and a bowl of olive oil, maybe, to dip the bread in. Some candles. Outside, the streets were oddly quiet, with everyone indoors beginning their festival supper. The occasional pair of feet ran by, as someone hurried to get home before sunset, before Passover began. Downstairs, a woman was singing Passover prayers.

No sooner had the friends set down their contribution of food on the rough wooden table and settled themselves on the benches to either side, than Jesus took off his robe and, carrying a basin of water, started to wash each man's feet.

"Don't do that, Lord!" they protested, embarrassed, tucking their feet hard under the bench. "That's a servant's job! At the very least, we should do it for you!"

"I'm doing this for you as an example of how you should behave towards each other. Soon you will understand, I hope, just how far a man must be prepared to humble himself, for the sake of his brothers." He slipped his arms into his robe, and came

For I have given you an example, that ye should do as I have done to you.
JOHN 13:15

THE LAST SUPPER

Jesus said unto him, Verily I say unto thee, That this night, before the cock crow, thou shalt deny me thrice.

MATTHEW 26:34

back to the table. "Love one another," he told them. "When I'm gone, love each other as much as I have loved you."

"Where are you going?" asked Peter.

"Somewhere you can't follow."

"I'd follow you anywhere!" declared Peter hotly.

Jesus shook his head. "No. No, you wouldn't, Peter. Before the cock crows, I know that three times you'll deny even knowing me ... Besides, I'm on my way to Heaven! And don't worry, Heaven's a big place: there'll be plenty of room there for you all, one day.

All of you. Even though tonight one of you will betray me."

"No!" There was uproar and confusion. A bench fell over, the dish of oil clattered to the floor.

"Who, me?"

"Not me!"

"Never!"

"Nor me!"

"Who do you mean, Lord?"

"Someone who has dipped his bread into the same bowl as I

THE LAST SUPPER

And he answered and said, He that dippeth his hand with me in the dish, the same shall betray me.
MATTHEW 26:23

And as they were eating, Jesus took bread, and blessed it, and brake it, and gave it to the disciples, and said, Take, eat; this is my body. And he took the cup, and gave thanks, and gave it to them, saying, Drink ye all of it; For this is my blood of the new testament, which is shed for many for the remission of sins.
MATTHEW 26: 26, 27, 28

have," said Jesus. That did not tell them much: there was only one dish of salt on the table.

But the bread in Judas Iscariot's mouth stuck in his gullet. Though he turned the salty lump over and over with his tongue, he could barely remember how to swallow. Silently, without drawing attention to himself, he got up and left the room.

Jesus picked up a loaf, gave thanks to God, and broke it into portions. "My body will be broken like this bread," he said. "Eat some, and remember me whenever you break bread in future." Then he poured wine into a cup. "My blood will be poured out like this wine, for the good of all humanity. Drink some, all of you, and remember me whenever you share a cup of wine. I won't taste wine again now, before my death."

Then, shocked and bewildered, they sang a prayer, and the meal came to an end. They did not go to bed, however, but outside into the dark, walking the short distance to the hill called Olivet. The trees rustled overhead, like wings. Tonight the Angel of Death would not be passing over; like little Zacchaeus, he sat waiting and watching in the branches. Waiting for Jesus.

IN THE GARDEN

JESUS HAD TAKEN, recently, to spending each night on Olivet hill, sleeping under the stars. Tonight he did not go there to sleep, but to pray. "Wait here for me," he said to the disciples, "and pray that God won't test your faith too far." He went a short way off, knelt down and prayed, and it was plain, even in the dark, that he was facing a terrible ordeal. His shoulders bent, his body rocked in agony, and the sweat fell from his face in drops like blood. "Father, don't ask me to drink from this cup of suffering . . . But let it be as you intend, not as I wish."

He walked back to the disciples. Perhaps he could hear the drone of Peter's snore as he dozed against an olive tree. "Asleep?" he asked agitatedly. "Wake up! Pray, for your own sakes!"

They tried, they really did. But three times they dozed off. "We want to keep awake, but our eyes just won't stay open!" The third time Jesus woke them, it was simply to say, "It's time."

The night's silence was broken by movement lower down the hill. People were coming, and not the soft-sandalled sick seeking healing, nor the crowds hungry for knowledge. These were armed men - the Temple guard!

What did they see, those guards, peering through the darkness? A group of unkempt men, similarly dressed? So which was Jesus? It would not do to arrest the wrong man. Still, they had taken precautions against that. "Go on, then. Point him out," they snarled at their paid informer.

"The one I kiss," said Judas Iscariot, and darting forwards, he went directly to Jesus, betraying him with a kiss on the cheek. The look Jesus turned on him made Judas's blood run cold in his veins and his heart weigh like a millstone within his chest. He broke away and ran from the garden, like Adam driven out of Eden.

Watch and pray, that ye enter not into temptation: the spirit indeed is willing, but the flesh is weak.
MATTHEW 26:41

Now he that betrayed him gave them a sign, saying, Whomsoever I shall kiss, that same is he: hold him fast.
MATTHEW 26:48

Sure of their man now, the guard closed in. There was a scuffle. Two of the disciples were carrying swords. The High Priest's slave gave a cry of pain and clutched at his ear. Blood dribbled down to the point of his chin.

"Enough!" said Jesus, and the confusion ceased. "Why?" he asked his ambushers. "Every day I came and went in the city. Why come after me here, at night, with swords and clubs like some robber?" Then he touched the slave's ear: it was healed at once.

Unmoved, the guard grabbed hold of Jesus - left the others, but hustled Jesus away, a prisoner. The disciples scattered, dazed and afraid, like sheep deprived of their shepherd. But Peter followed on, at a distance, all the way to the High Priest's house. There was a bonfire burning in the yard, and round it sat various early risers, excited by the commotion. "He's one of them," said a maid, pointing at Peter. "Ask him what happened."

"Who? Me? Not me," said Peter, and moved sharply out of the firelight. At the gate, he collided with a man, who peered into his face. "You're one of *his* men, aren't you?"

"Whose? Don't know the man." And he stumbled away, half running, expecting at any moment a heavy hand to fall on his shoulder and for him to be arrested too. The bright light of dawn burned like a hot wire along the rim of the sky. The city was restless. A hand grabbed Peter's robe. "He's one of them! A Galilean like him!"

"I don't know what you're talking about. Let go of me!"

In the distance, a cock crowed. Jesus's words came back as plainly as if he were speaking in Peter's ear: "Before the cock crows, I know that three times you'll deny even knowing me." Peter pressed his forehead to a wall and wept with self-loathing.

And again he denied with an oath, I do not know the man.
MATTHEW 26:72

And Peter remembered the word of Jesus, which said unto him, Before the cock crow, thou shalt deny me thrice. And he went out, and wept bitterly.
MATTHEW 26:75

JESUS ON TRIAL

HAVING ARRESTED JESUS, the Temple authorities had to find him guilty of something. The more innocent he proved under interrogation, the more thwarted they felt, and the more they hated him. So they beat him and humiliated him, covered his eyes with a blindfold, then asked, as they struck him, "Who hit you, prophet? Don't you know?" Their own cruelty rebounded and made them more cruel than ever. "Are you the Saviour prophesied in the Scriptures?" they kept asking.

"You wouldn't believe me if I said I was," Jesus replied.

"Are you the Son of God?"

"You said it, not I," Jesus replied. In short, he said nothing which gave them any grounds to execute him - and yet every time he spoke, they threw up their hands and cried, "Listen to him! He deserves to die!"

Then said they all, Art thou then the Son of God? And he said unto them, Ye say that I am.

LUKE 22:70

The Temple court had no power to put a man to death. So they sent him on to Pontius Pilate, governor of the region. Pilate despised their petty squabbling and wanted nothing to do with the whole nasty business. It did not seem to him that Jesus had done anything wrong. So, ducking the responsibility, he sent Jesus on to be tried by the Roman authorities, in the person of Herod Antipas.

Now Herod had heard quite a lot about Jesus, and had a secret hankering to meet the famous preacher and miracle-worker. He would have liked to see a miracle or two, hear a sample of ringing rhetoric. When Jesus kept silent, Herod was disappointed - he found no entertainment in him, and sent him straight back to Pilate.

"Look," said Pilate wearily, "I've tried this man and find him innocent of any crime. So does Herod." The Temple elders looked back at him with pursed lips. Outside, crowds had gathered in the streets.

Once a year, on the feast of Passover, Pilate traditionally released one prisoner from the city dungeons to please the people. Suddenly he glimpsed a solution to his problem. Why not give the crowds outside a chance to rescue their hero - the man they had cheered to the sky's rafters only days before? So he asked the crowds, from his open window, "Why don't I just beat this fellow and grant him his freedom, in the tradition of Passover?"

But the Temple plotters were way ahead of him. They had already sent agitators in among the crowds, whispering, persuading, poisoning hearts and minds . . . A crowd thinks with a single mind - like a flock of sheep. And with their shepherd gone, the crowds who had flocked to hear Jesus were led astray with breathtaking ease.

"*Free Barabbas!*" they chanted. (The traders driven out of the Temple shouted loudest of all.) "*Free Barabbas!*"

"The murderer?"

"Yes! Give us Barabbas! We want Barabbas!"

"Then what shall I do with the man Jesus?" asked Pilate, bewildered by their mindless venom.

"*Crucify him! Crucify him!*" shouted the people, the selfsame crowds who had strewn palm leaves in Jesus's path and cried "Hosanna!" as he rode into Jerusalem.

Pontius Pilate called for a bowl and water, and washed his hands, in plain view of the crowds. "Do as you like with him. You see: his blood is not on my hands."

If only it were really that easy to wash off responsibility for our actions.

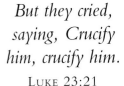

But they cried, saying, Crucify him, crucify him.
LUKE 23:21

When Pilate saw that he could prevail nothing, but that rather a tumult was made, he took water and washed his hands before the multitude, saying, I am innocent of the blood of this just person: see ye to it. Then answered all the people, and said, His blood be on us, and on our children.
MATTHEW 27: 24, 25

THE CRUCIFIXION

"LET HIS BLOOD be on us and on our children!" ranted the crowds, and Pontius Pilate gave them what they wanted – a death sentence. It was safer that way. The so-called "King of the Jews" would no longer present a threat to all-powerful Caesar, and Caesar would be left in no doubt as to Pilate's loyalty.

The palace guards flogged Jesus, then dressed him up in mock splendour – a purple robe and a crown – spitting and jeering, "Hail, King of the Jews!" The crown was plaited out of thorns, so that drops of blood ran like tears down his face.

Then they brought him his cross – the wooden instrument of torture on which he was to die. A triangular notice was fixed to it, by order of Pilate, saying, *This is the King of the Jews.*

"You can't put that!" complained the chief priests. "Write, 'This man *says* he is the King of the . . .' "

"What I have written, I have written," said Pilate.

Jesus was already too weak to carry his cross out of the city, all the way to the place of execution. A man in the watching crowd was ordered to help him – a foreigner, an outsider called Simon. Picture that dreadful procession: Jesus and Simon, with two robbers, also condemned to die, the huge, crossed slats of heavy wood, the onlookers, some spiteful, some just curious, the disciples hanging back fearfully at a distance. There are the families of the condemned men, weeping and desolate, and some of the sick people Jesus cured, sickened once again by the sight of his suffering. And there are the iron-faced guards to whom this is just another execution.

Crucifixion. It was not an unusual sight. The Romans in particular thought it set a stern example to common criminals. On the crest of Golgotha Hill, which rears up like a gigantic

THE CRUCIFIXION

And he bearing his cross went forth into a place called the place of a skull, which is called in the Hebrew Golgotha: Where they crucified him, and two other with him, on either side one, and Jesus in the midst.
JOHN 19:17, 18

And he said unto Jesus, Lord, remember me when thou comest into thy kingdom. And Jesus said unto him, Verily I say unto thee, Today shalt thou be with me in paradise.
LUKE 23:42, 43

skull, the soldiers nailed Jesus by his hands and feet to the crude wooden cross-tree. They must have leaned low over him, those men with their hammers and nails - must have done the messy job a dozen times before and grown hardened to the screams, the curses, the vile language, the hopeless pleas for mercy. All Jesus said as they nailed him to the cross was, "Father, forgive them; they don't realize what they are doing." And that the guards had never heard before.

"If you're the Son of God, come down! Save yourself!" jeered the crowd, baring their teeth in jackal grins as the cross was dropped home jarringly into a socket in the parched ground.

"Aren't you supposed to be the Saviour?" howled one of the robbers. "Save yourself and us with you, why don't you?"

The other robber silenced him. "Have some respect, will you? We had this coming to us. But this man - he's done nothing wrong! . . . Jesus, remember me when you're crowned King of Heaven."

Jesus turned his head awkwardly and smiled. "I promise you: today we'll be together in Paradise, you and I."

He said very little else. From noon till three the sky turned black, as though the sun had closed up its eye sooner than see the sorry sight. When Jesus was thirsty, someone ran to fetch him a drink of cheap, sour wine. But no dove flew out of Heaven, no beam of sunlight blessed Jesus with its kiss. No voice spoke out of the clouds. At three o'clock, Jesus cried aloud, "My God! My God, why have you abandoned me?"

Soon afterwards, he spoke again: "It is finished. Father, into your hands I entrust my spirit."

Down in the city, in the heart of the silent Temple, the curtain which veiled the Holiest of Holy Jewish shrines from the eyes of ordinary people ripped from top to bottom. The earth shook and crazed, buildings and people staggered. Jerusalem was full of screaming. Then silence. Jesus was dead.

A Roman soldier flung against the foot of the cross by the earth tremor looked up, his eyes full of horror. "Truly, this man was the Son of God!"

To him fell the task of ensuring that the prisoners were really dead before their bodies were taken down from the crosses. He sank a spear into Jesus's side, and was splashed by a stream of blood, thin blood diluted with water. *"Let his blood be on us and on our children!"* the crowds had ranted. But surely they had not meant this, this fountain of forgiveness, this spring of tenderness, this splash of red love falling on a darkened world.

THE CRUCIFIXION

And when Jesus had cried with a loud voice, he said, Father, into thy hands I commend my spirit: and having said thus, he gave up the ghost.
Luke 23:46

AN OPENING OF EYES

"I SHOULD NEVER HAVE DONE IT! I destroyed an innocent man!" Judas Iscariot cried, and threw down the thirty pieces of silver he had been paid to betray Christ.

"What's that to us?" The chief priests looked back at him from under hooded lids: They had what they wanted. Judas ran from the place — ran and ran, but could not outrun his agony of guilt, and killed himself before nightfall.

And he took it down, and wrapped it in linen, and laid it in a sepulchre that was hewn in stone, wherein never man before was laid.
LUKE 23:53

Men crucified as criminals had no right to a grave. But a certain rich man called Joseph had heard Jesus preach and could not bear to see the corpse left for birds to peck at. He plucked up courage and begged Pilate's permission to take it down from the cross. Pilate said yes. Joseph wrapped the mangled body in linen and laid it in a tomb he had bought for himself. The rock tomb was sealed with a huge round stone, very well sealed — the authorities made sure of that.

All this happened so quickly that there was no chance for Jesus' mother, or any of the other womenfolk among his friends, to anoint his body fittingly. (For thirty years, Mary had owned a pot of precious myrrh for that very purpose; it had been given to her by a wise man, a present for her newborn son.) The next day was the Sabbath, when nothing could be done. So it was the third day from the crucifixion before Mary and her friend Mary Magdalene could visit the tomb. To their horror, they found it vandalized: the stone had been rolled back and there was no sign of a body!

And they found the stone rolled away from the sepulchre.
LUKE 24:2

Mary Magdalene ran, ran to fetch Simon Peter and John, and after telling them the terrible news, trailed slowly behind them back to the graveyard.

Simon Peter ran, but John ran faster. He got to the place

first . . . but hadn't the nerve to enter. Peering inside, he saw the linen grave-clothes lying flat, as though the body inside had simply melted away. Peter, when he came panting along, did not hesitate but ducked right inside the gloomy tomb.

What did he think of what he saw? Did he realize at once what had happened? Did he and John believe then and there - or did they reel away home confused and bewildered? Certainly they barely spoke a word to Mary Magdalene, for she was left sobbing helplessly outside the empty tomb. She too stooped and looked in.

It was not empty at all!

Two men - two strangers dressed all in white - sat where Jesus's body had lain. "Why are you crying?" they asked cheerfully.

"Because they've taken my Jesus away and I don't know where!"

"Who are you looking for?" asked a voice behind her. She turned, but her eyes were too full of sun-dazzled tears to see clearly. She thought the silhouette must be the gardener's.

AN OPENING OF EYES

Then went in also that other disciple, which came first to the sepulchre, and he saw, and believed. For as yet they knew not the scripture, that he must rise again from the dead.
JOHN 20:8, 9

*And when he had
so said, he shewed
unto them his
hands and his side.
Then were the
disciples glad, when
they saw the Lord.
Then said Jesus to
them again, Peace
be unto you: as my
Father hath sent
me, even so send
I you.*
JOHN 20:20, 21

"Oh please, sir, if it was you, tell me where you've put him, and I'll take him away!"

Then the man said, "Mary." It was Jesus: his face, his body, his hands. Mary reached out adoring hands. "No. Don't touch me. Just go and tell the others: I'm on my way home – to my Father and yours, to my God and your God."

Tell them? She bellowed it in their ears. She danced it round the room, laughing and crying all at once. Maybe Peter and John believed her, but the rest of the disciples? Well, they probably wanted so much to believe that they did not dare. That evening ten of them were crowded together in one house, behind locked doors. Jesus might or might not be alive, but one fact was certain: the authorities had killed him and would like to kill them as well.

All of a sudden, there he was. No knock at the door, no white lightning. Jesus simply stood there, saying, "Peace." And when he held up his hands, the lamplight shone through the holes the nails had gouged in his palms.

TIME TOGETHER

ONE DISCIPLE called Thomas, was not there that night in the locked house. When the others told him how Jesus had appeared, he did not believe a word of it. "Not unless I see with my own eyes – see, touch, everything!" he retorted. "Wishful thinking!"

Eight days later, when the same thing happened, and Jesus appeared to all eleven men, he went straight up to Thomas and invited him to touch the scars of those terrible wounds. (Even when he was not present, Jesus knew everything that happened.) "Better to believe without proof, though," warned Jesus, as Thomas hopped about, speechless with joy, shame and embarrassment.

Next time the disciples saw Jesus, they were almost too busy to notice. Five of them were having a particularly bad night's fishing – not so much as a sand eel in the nets all night long. Isn't there always someone, at a time like that, telling you that you are doing it all wrong, offering helpful advice? Sure enough, a man on the shadowy shoreline called, "Not caught anything yet?"

"Not a thing."

"Let your nets down on the other side, then!"

Oho yes. Such a difference *that* was going to make! To shift to a piece of water five paces from the first! They did it, though.

And the net filled up with fish – shoals of silvery fish so heavy that the net could hardly be dragged on board. The sun was rising out of the sea, turning the shoreline blue and gold, making it easier to see clearly. "It's Jesus!" cried John, pointing to the figure on the beach.

At that, Peter leapt over the side, wading ashore through a bow-wave of flying spray. By the time the boat beached, Jesus had lit a fire and cooked a breakfast of fish which they shared. It

And Thomas answered and said unto him, My Lord and my God. Jesus saith unto him, Thomas, because thou hast seen me, thou hast believed: blessed are they that have not seen, and yet have believed.
JOHN 20: 28, 29

And he said unto them, Cast the net on the right side of the ship, and ye shall find. They cast therefore, and now they were not able to draw it for the multitude of fishes.
JOHN 21:6

He saith unto him the third time, Simon, son of Jonas, lovest thou me? Peter was grieved because he said unto him the third time, Lovest thou me? And he said unto him, Lord, thou knowest all things; thou knowest that I love thee. Jesus saith unto him, Feed my sheep.

JOHN 21:17

was a meal infinitely more delicious than their Passover supper, salty with the sea instead of with tears.

"Do you love me, Peter?" Jesus asked all of a sudden. Three times he asked it, for all Peter kept vowing that he did.

"You *know* I love you, Lord!" he protested a third time.

"Then feed my sheep." It was an awesome commission: to care for Jesus's followers in his place, to guide and encourage them. "You're a free man at the moment," Jesus warned him, "but when you're old, people will take your freedom away - even your life."

But Peter was ready now to die for Jesus's sake: his courage had failed him once, never again.

They all learned a lot from Jesus in those wonderful days after he rose from the dead. They grew from uneducated fishermen and labourers into preachers and leaders of men. But Jesus could not stay on with them. He was, as he had told Mary, on his way home.

One day he took them all to Bethany, where they had spent such happy times together. "All power in Earth and Heaven has been put into my hands," he said. "Now I am sending *you* out to make disciples of all the world."

"But how . . . ?"

"When, will you . . . ?"

"You can't just . . ." There was so much they wanted to know.

"Wait. I shall send you a companion to give you the strength you need . . . And anyway, I shall be with you, always, till the end of the world." As he raised his hands in blessing, Jesus was hidden from them by tatters of cloud snagging the hillside.

Two men - two strangers dressed all in white, who surely had not been there a moment before - asked why everyone was staring up into the sky.

"Our friend . . . Our master . . ." began Simon Peter, barely able to speak.

"Don't you know he'll come back the same way he left? One of these days?" they said. Then the strangers, too, were swallowed up by the mist.

Go ye therefore, and teach all nations, baptizing them in the name of the Father, and of the Son, and of the Holy Ghost . . . and, lo, I am with you alway, even unto the end of the world. Amen.
MATTHEW 28:19, 20

THE GODSEND

W HAT WERE THEY WAITING FOR? "Wait," Jesus had told them, but what for, and for how long? The disciples met every day, talking, praying . . . waiting, but it was hard to imagine what could replace Jesus in their lives.

About six weeks after Passover when Jesus had died, another annual festival - Pentecost - brought Jews flocking to Jerusalem. This time they were celebrating the time when, on a lonely mountain top shrouded in cloud, God gave to Moses the Holy Law by which the Jewish nation was to live.

On Pentecost itself, the disciples were together, as usual, talking, no doubt, of the new commandment Jesus had given them - to love one another. Suddenly all the doors were banging, the hangings flapping, the whole house howling with a wild, whirling wind. The wind was not from the north, or the south, east or west, but blew out of the sky like a rainless cloudburst - and borne along in it were rags and tatters of fire! When the wind dropped, a single flame still hovered over each man's head.

And suddenly there came a sound from heaven as of a rushing mighty wind, and it filled all the house where they were sitting. And there appeared unto them cloven tongues like as of fire, and it sat upon each of them. And they were all filled with the Holy Ghost, and began to speak with other tongues, as the Spirit gave them utterance.
ACTS 2:2, 3, 4

But the *real* fire burned *inside* them. They were filled with an ecstasy of joy, whooping and laughing and shouting out, "Praise be! Praise Christ Jesus! Thank you, God, for this - this - *happiness*!" Within each breast, resting against each heart was a sublime contentment and strength, an invisible companion to which they gave the name "Holy Spirit".

"What's all the noise about? What's going on?" Passersby heard the clamour and a crowd began to gather outside as in the good old days of Jesus's teaching. There were Parthians and Medes, Libyans and Egyptians, Romans and Greeks in that crowd. But oddly enough, every man and woman heard the disciples praising God in his or her own language.

"Are they drunk, or what?" asked someone, unnerved.

"No, we're not drunk," said Peter in a loud, calm voice full of authority. "It's simply a prophecy coming true. You remember the Scripture? 'I will pour out my Spirit on all of you; your young people will see visions and your old men dream dreams.' It's the beginning. The beginning of God's Kingdom on Earth!"

A great many people heard about Christ that day who had never heard Jesus himself preach - never even seen him in person. Three thousand believed what Peter (and the Holy Spirit) had to say. Those three thousand told others, those others told more, and so the word began to spread like the ripples on a pool, spreading always wider: Jesus Christ had died, but was alive again, and his family was getting bigger every day.

THE GODSEND

BEAUTIFUL GATES

JOHN AND SIMON PETER went about as a team, missing no opportunity to tell people about Jesus. One day, beside the Temple entrance known as the "Beautiful Gate", a crippled beggar asked them for money. Asked them, who never knew quite where the next meal was coming from. Peter replied, "I have no silver or gold, but I'll give you what I do have: in the name of Jesus, walk!"

The man felt his legs grow strong - legs which had been as limp and lifeless as old cord - strong enough to dance and leap and run. That brought the crowds swarming round, for everyone knew the beggar very well - a familiar ugliness at the foot of the Beautiful Gate. But as they listened to Peter, he opened to them a gate more beautiful than that which towered over them: he showed them the way to reach God through Jesus Christ, His son.

It vexed the Temple elders past endurance. Had they got rid of Jesus to have to put up with this? Peter and John were strictly forbidden to preach "in the name of Jesus Christ". But what did the disciples care? They took no notice. They were discovering the power and joy of having the Holy Spirit within them, and no threats or punishments could quench that incandescent fire.

More people became disciples every day, throwing aside their old lifestyles and working out a new way to live. They formed a community, pooling all their money and possessions and sharing them out equally. Not everyone left behind their old shortcomings - some still lapsed into greed, pride, quarrelling. But they were only learning, after all, learning how to lead a different, better kind of life. And that always takes time.

Then Peter said, Silver and gold have I none; but such as I have give I thee: In the name of Jesus Christ of Nazareth rise up and walk.

ACTS 3:6

SEEING THE LIGHT

THE HARDSHIPS DID NOT STOP at threats or beatings. The bigger the new community grew, the more angry the orthodox Jewish leaders became. In an effort to stamp out this new "cult", they began to persecute believers brutally, putting them in prison – even putting them to death.

No one was more ruthless than a man called Saul. He searched far and wide for Christians to arrest and drag back to Jerusalem for trial. He was on just such a mission to the city of Damascus, when the truth literally stopped him in his tracks.

A flash of light so bright that it stung his eyes and rocked his brain felled Saul to the ground.

Finding himself still alive, he rose gingerly on to hands and

SEEING THE LIGHT

And he fell to the earth, and heard a voice saying unto him, Saul, Saul, why persecutest thou me?

ACTS 9:4

And immediately there fell from his eyes as it had been scales: and he received sight forthwith, and arose, and was baptized.

ACTS 9:18

knees, flinching as a voice spoke loudly, close by. *"Saul! Saul! Why are you persecuting me?"*

The men with Saul heard the voice, too, but could see no one. The question seemed to hang in the air, like the clash of a cymbal, but who could have spoken it?

Saul could see no one. Saul could see no one and nothing. The lightning had seared his eyeballs, sealed the pupils, robbed him of daylight. He was stone blind.

His servants led him into Damascus, and for three days he sat in despair, refusing to eat, praying for understanding. He had never acted out of malice - only devout belief in the Jewish law, in Jewish orthodoxy. Why should God punish him for cleansing the Jewish community of this new cult? For doing his zealous duty?

There was a knock at the door. A man came in, introducing himself as Ananias. He was patently frightened, for he was a Christian and knew Saul's reputation. But he came, even so. "Is there a man here called Saul of Tarsus? The Lord has sent me to give him back his sight." So saying, he laid his hands over Saul's eyes.

Now Saul, imprisoned in his cocoon of dark, must have done a great deal of thinking about that light, that voice on the road. When Ananias took away his hands, Saul blinked in the sudden brightness, blinked up into Ananias's face with eyes which could see again! "He's the Son of God, isn't he? Jesus is the Son of God."

And that is what he took into the synagogues of Damascus: not threats or warrants, but a fiercer belief in Jesus than almost any other Christian. He changed his name to Paul, and poured more energy into spreading the faith than ever he had spent trying to stamp it out. He determined to tell the whole Mediterranean world the good news about Jesus. Wherever he went, his words struck home like a bolt of lightning, and the letters he sent as he travelled make hair-raising reading. For he scrambled from one danger to the next, holding his life in his teeth, trying to spread word of Jesus as fast and as far as he could through a hostile world.

TO THE ENDS OF THE EARTH

LIKE THE RIPPLES spreading outwards from a splash, word of Jesus spread towards the edges of the Roman Empire. Wherever Paul or Peter went, things seemed to be made easy for them: someone stood waiting with an open door, a cooked meal . . . When Peter was put in prison, an angel came at midnight and freed him. When Paul was imprisoned, an earthquake shook open every lock and manacle, and he walked free. They worked miracles, too, and some people mistook them for gods.

Equally, the hardships grew greater every day. They were stoned, beaten, put in the stocks and into prison. Friends were killed. Paul was tried by church courts, civil courts – so many courts! And each trial he used as an opportunity to speak about Jesus. But finally Paul was shuffled away into a prison cell for years on end, his case continually under review, never settled. So just for a change, he made the Roman law work in his favour, and demanded to be "tried by Caesar". That was his right, as a Roman citizen. And it would give him a chance to speak of Christ in Rome – Rome! – the very centre of the Roman world.

Under military escort, Paul was put aboard a ship bound for the Italian coast. Some of his friends paid to sail too, and keep

But the angel of the Lord by night opened the prison doors, and brought them forth, and said, Go, stand and speak in the temple to the people all the words of this life.
ACTS 5:19, 20

Paul company. It was late in the year to be sailing; most ships rested up during the rough winter weather.

"Don't go on," said Paul, when the sky began to cloud over and the sea turned surly. "This voyage is doomed." But no one paid him any heed. What did he know, a landlubber and convict?

When the storm struck, it stripped the boat of her sails and lashed her with spiteful waves. It kicked her off the sea lanes and beat her till her boards split. The crew threw cargo and tackle overboard just to keep her afloat. Day and night were indistinguishable, for sun and moon were hidden by the pall of cloud. Sailors and passengers despaired of ever seeing dry land again.

Not Paul. "I did warn you," he pointed out, annoyingly. "But don't worry. Every one will get safely ashore. God has told me as much." They looked at him through slicked hair, faces streaming, their eyelashes heavy with rain; too tired to throw him overboard.

As daylight faded, the ship's lead line touched bottom: the water was getting shallower! The crew wanted to abandon ship, knowing land must be somewhere near. But Paul calmly suggested a bite to eat instead. "Wait till morning! You've eaten nothing for days. Come on, eat! Drink! We'll all feel better."

And they did.

Dawn revealed a sandy, inviting cove, islanders running to and fro pointing at the ship. Safety! But a sandbar just then stove in the ship's hull, the swell broke her back, and the waves began pulling her apart. "Shall we kill the prisoners?" asked a guard, staggering on the listing deck.

"No. Every man for himself," said Centurion Julian, officer-in-charge; he had developed a sneaking admiration for Paul.

Every man jack got ashore from that wreck, just as Paul had said they would. They waded ashore on to a Maltese beach to be warmed and fed by the friendly locals.

As Paul helped make a bonfire, a snake slid from the kindling and battened itself round his wrist: a deadly, green bracelet.

*And he shook off
the beast into the
fire, and felt
no harm.*
ACTS 28:5

*And he that taketh
not his cross and
followeth after me,
is not worthy of
me. He that
findeth his life shall
lose it: and he that
loseth his life for
my sake shall
find it.*
MATTHEW 10:38, 39

"Aha! Justice catching up with the wrongdoer," said those who saw it. "Clearly the gods didn't mean *that* one to escape punishment for his crimes. Be dead in a few minutes."

But Paul did not die. He just shook the snake off his wrist, and sat down to eat, as though nothing had happened.

It was a season outside time, that winter in Malta. The storms put an end to shipping; the voyage to Rome could not continue. Centurion Julian and his soldiers and the Maltese people got to know Paul and his friends, listened to his teaching, brought their sick to him and saw them healed. For three happy months that prison ship lay in harbour. Then spring came and Paul was obliged to continue on his way, to be tried in Rome.

The Christians already living in Rome, greeted him more like a celebrity than a convict. He had written them so many inspiring letters that they felt they already knew him. And they made sure he did not moulder in some dank Roman prison cell, either. Held under house arrest, he could not freely come and go, but that did not stop him preaching, writing, conducting worship - and in Rome! At the very heart of the Roman Empire!

What became of him? Or of Peter? They disappear from the pages of history and were very probably killed for their faith. Many of Rome's emperors tried to wipe out Christianity by killing every Christian. But then Herod tried to kill the infant Christ, didn't he? And Pontius Pilate tried to put an end to him at Golgotha. The powerful will always try to crush great ideas and heroes who cast too long a shadow.

If Paul and Peter were put to death, dying held no fears for them. And they passed out of history no further than Jesus when he stepped behind that low cloud. For they knew Jesus had defeated death once and for all. It would be just one more moment's suffering on the hard road to Heaven, then they would reach a crest in the road, glimpse the Kingdom of God, and someone familiar, his scarred hand raised in welcome.

VISIONS

THE LAST BOOK of the Bible was written by a man called John. Some say it was the same John who knew Jesus: the man who called himself "the disciple Jesus loved". Certainly he was an exile, imprisoned on an island. Certainly Jesus loved him. For he appeared to John in a vision, and allowed him to glimpse, in his imagination, the whole of Space and Time.

John wrote down his vision: the last days of the world, a fearful time followed by a final triumphant battle. He wrote in pictures: monstrous dragons, hideous beasts and superhuman figures in a fantastic landscape. On one level, his book was a coded message full of secret symbols to a few like-minded Christians. John had to use numbers, passwords, symbols, for he could not speak out plainly in those times of persecution. And the people who read it would have understood: this beast represents the Emperor, say, or this the Roman Empire. We can only look at it now like some treasure map found floating in a bottle; we have no key to the riddle.

And yet the map still works! A treasure is still waiting for those who can find it. Part of John's vision is timeless.

I am Alpha and Omega, the beginning and the ending, saith the Lord, which is, and which was, and which is to come, the Almighty.
REVELATION 1:8

And I saw a new heaven and a new earth: for the first heaven and the first earth were passed away; and there was no more sea. And I John saw the holy city, new Jerusalem, coming down from God out of heaven, prepared as a bride adorned for her husband.
REVELATION 21:1, 2

VISIONS

And the city had no need of the sun, neither of the moon, to shine in it: for the glory of God did lighten it, and the Lamb is the light thereof. And the nations of them which are saved shall walk in the light of it: and the kings of the earth do bring their glory and honour into it. And the gates of it shall not be shut at all by day: for there shall be no night there.

REVELATION 21:23, 24, 25

For the world still seems to be in the grip of tyrants and fiends endlessly powerful and wicked – every bit as terrifying as horned beasts from the sea or dragons with many heads. The four pale horsemen: War, Disease, Starvation, Death, are still galloping over the planet, pitiless, unstoppable. The world seems to be hurtling towards its own wilful destruction . . .

Then suddenly, in comes Christ!

In his vision, John first saw Jesus as a helpless lamb going to its death as a holy sacrifice, to pay for the sins of humankind. Later he saw a bridegroom arriving for a wedding: the faithful bride (the Church) has sat waiting so long for him – the ultimate love, the ultimate friend – but now they can celebrate the endless happiness ahead. His angels have cut to pieces the demons, the beasts, the monsters. God has judged between the good and the bad, and the Earth is transformed by his blazing, marvellous presence.

There is no more night: Jesus is light itself.

There are no more tears: every sadness is over.

No more death, no more regret, no more wrong.

Is it a picture of the end of the world? Must we wait until the stars fall and the sun implodes and the planets unthread and spill, spinning away, before Christ returns?

Or has John's "Revelation" also got something to say about how Jesus blazes his way into the life of a believer, conquering demons, ousting fear, offering rescue, promising everlasting joy, filling the imagination with visions of Paradise?